A Message
for the
Millennium

A MESSAGE
FOR THE
MILLENNIUM

K. Martin-Kuri

With an introduction
by Terry Lynn Taylor

BALLANTINE BOOKS
NEW YORK

Library of Congress Cataloging-in-Publication Data
Martin-Kuri, K.
A message for the millennium / K. Martin-Kuri.
p.   cm.
ISBN 0-345-39522-0
1. Angels. 2. Spiritual life. I. Title.
BL477.M365 1996
291.2'15—dc20   95-46625
                                                                        CIP

Text design by Holly Johnson

Manufactured in the United States of America

First Edition: February 1996

10 9 8 7 6 5 4 3 2 1

This book is dedicated
with love
to all those who listen.

*He that is of God
heareth God's words.*
—JOHN 8:47

Contents

Acknowledgments

You are able to read this book because I received some special assistance for which I am deeply grateful. I would like to acknowledge Joëlle Delbourgo, my editor at Ballantine, for her ability to recognize the importance of the message; my literary agent from heaven, Loretta Barrett; Leigh Ann Sackrider for her sensitive support and skill; Gary Morris for his patient attentiveness.

Also, Terry Lynn Taylor for her friendship and continuous encouragement to me to offer the message to the public; Janine Bjork for her loving generosity of soul; my personal copy editor, Barbara Nye Carter; H. Smith, who surrounds the work with his continuous prayers; Diane Carter Shiflett for her Christimbued selfless loyalty; Shirley Law for fidelity to the angels; and Susie Warren Stewart for help in rewrites and happy times.

I would like to acknowledge the people who have supported my career throughout my life, from the collectors of the paintings I produced to every volunteer who helped with the work of the angels.

I would be remiss, however, if I did not remember, as well, the loving sacrifices of my two best friends, who sat beside me each day and often into the night. They were ever faithful and rarely complained that their master seemed to be permanently placed in a chair before a computer. One is a little sheltie dog named Ani (spirit angel) and the other is a Siamese cat called Time. I know that on many occasions the support from the heavens came through the love of these two friends.

Foreword

I have been waiting ten years for this book. When the angel book market began to explode, K. Martin-Kuri withheld her offering because she believed messages have their own appointed time for delivery.

When I read the manuscript, I felt a heightened perception of beauty and light come over me, the same stirrings that happen when I know the angels are near. The material in the book expanded my knowledge about angels and our relationship to them. After reading it, I made a very big change in my life. I gave up something that I finally realized was not aligned with my spiritual commitment to help the heavens. I am very grateful that in this book great truths are finally told for humanity.

I know that to write this book required much courage because of its strong message to all peoples of the world that it is time to change our way of thinking and our lifestyles. We are close to annihiliation on many levels if we continue to travel the path that we are now on. The angels of God want to help us, but first we must ask God for their assistance. I think this book is an answer to the problems that confront us.

This is a unique book. It is not one you read once and put on the shelf. You will find that each time you read it, the important messages will become more pronounced.

One such message is that, in our civilization, deterioration in the sense of individual responsibility has reached the proportions of a major plague. We must face our crucial role in saving life from the opposing forces of darkness. The call is not to destroy the gifts of technology and science which are part of the global crises but to transform the forces by recognition and proper use.

It is also time for us to lift the obstacles of false thinking that we allow to stand in the way of receiving true heavenly nourishment, as discussed in chapter six on the difficult subject of money. I especially like the concept given in the revelation that our attitude and practices with money have caused a major hindrance to the angels of God in giving us the nourishment we need individually and globally.

Years ago K. Martin-Kuri warmly accepted my proffered friendship and respect. She graciously received my profuse compliments about her art and her work, which truly comes from angelic realms. For the first time I knew that I had found someone from whom I could learn and with whom I could also share my love for the heavens.

Karyn has become a valued, consistent friend and has guided me through some very crucial moments with her direct way of helping me to see the truth with the lightness of humor and with love. She has an unbelievably strong faith in God, and this faith is the directing source that has enabled her to withstand the blows of human existence. This faith has changed many people and inspired them to go forward on their spiritual path. Strength of soul has allowed her to meet the extraordinary demands of her life work, which she actually does with a quiet inner humility that shines from her soul.

As you discover more about K. Martin-Kuri, you will find that she is real, conscientious, and caring, always willing to assist others. Because she is a very private person, few know the depth of her involvement with the heavens. Know that you are not alone when you encounter the truths in this book. Karyn is praying for each soul who reads her words.

This book demands a lot of the reader. Our times require it. Do not ignore it. Let us heed this true message for the millennium. Remember to read between the lines with your heart and you will experience the deep sense of love that only the angels transmit from God.

—*Terry Lynn Taylor*

Introduction

This book actually started one day over forty years ago when I was a little girl. What happened to me on that day became the motivation for my life, all the research, and the long years filled with faithful perseverance. It has colored everything I do in the name of God.

What happened on that day was both natural for me and yet overwhelming. It began as I walked across our beautiful lawn on my way to school. (I was in first grade.) I heard lovely music in back of me, up in the air. Without turning around, I was able to see with my soul and spirit the veils of heaven open behind me, with millions and millions of angels gathered between earth and the Godhead. I fell to my knees and began to weep with the extraordinary beauty of what I experienced. Tears came also because I realized how much I loved that realm. I understood the meaning of what was being shown to me, and I knew there was a lifetime before me when I would often agonize between the ecstasy of God and the difficulties of day-to-day living.

I knew at that moment it was possible for human suffering on the earth to be transformed if humanity remembered the love and the help of God available through the angelic hierarchies. And so began my life's work.

For years I have preferred to share my offerings verbally and, as a painter, visually. It is now time to enter a new phase through use of the written word. It is much harder to communicate with you this way because I must paint in words, and the lights in our eyes cannot meet. It is quite difficult to translate the mysteries of heaven into words. Perhaps our hearts can unite, however, through the spirit behind the words themselves.

I think you will find that this book is quite different from any other on the subject of angels because it goes beyond just a discussion of angels. It explains the problems of human existence that heaven is urgently asking us to address, both as individuals and as a global community, if we are to make it safely through the new millennium.

In these pages, I emphasize the involvement of free will in the relationship between angels and humanity. Even the section on requests from heaven is built on the foundation of free will that can never be violated by the good angels. This means that the heavens are aware that you may choose to refuse the suggestions for change even if it would be for the betterment of our life here on earth.

It will become evident that up to this point humanity has not exercised its free will sufficiently to overcome the negative influences of rebellious angels that are destroying our society. This book is unusual because it provides cosmic clarity in a practical way to the behind-the-scenes battles between the forces of darkness and the angels of God over the human soul.

The time is upon us to develop new ways to act in response to the threat from the angels of darkness. They are leading us to an imminent abyss. To achieve this we need a shift of focus from the appearance of angels to the message they bring. We need to take the message seriously and accept the help of our Creator before it is too late.

Angels do not belong to any particular religion. If the world's religions recognized today that angels are everywhere, in cathedrals, churches, temples, mosques, tents, teepees, houses, and open air, we would have a common denominator upon which we could all agree. As you read this book your own religious life, whatever it is, should be enhanced. And for those of you who have a more general spiritual approach, this book will expand your connection to the heavens.

There is a wonderful secret that you might appreciate knowing while you read this book. Your angel will actually share the experience with you and has the power to clarify the thoughts that are important for your life. Some passages may be more difficult than others. Some require rereading a few times and others you might want to share with your friends. I recommend that along with reading you take time for prayer and inner work. Moments for serious contemplation or meditation will only enrich your experience.

One of the questions that may arise while you read is: where did it all come from? I believe you will have your answer after completing the book, without my explanation. What I will say, however, is that I have spent a lifetime working for the angels of God in one way or another. This experience has taught me that the focus should be on any message that is given to humanity rather than on the one who makes the delivery.

This book is a promise to you from the higher worlds that the heavens will open to you personally if you will choose to open your consciousness. The angels of God seek to lift your heart, your mind, and your soul as never before and share with you the glory that is beyond your wildest dreams. Heaven is waiting for you to accept the offer and receive the blessings.

May your life be surrounded in goodness and light while you read this book and may each page be nourishment for your soul now and in the times to come.

A Message
for the
Millennium

Chapter One

THE SITUATION

Since the moment of our creation in the cosmos, angels have called to humanity. They encourage us to always remember the Divine purpose and to seek that which is of the highest good. The angelic hierarchies are custodians of special memories. They are older than the planet Earth. The angels helped to weave the human spirit from Divine Substance. Throughout the process of universal creation, these heavenly beings have served the will of God in protecting and guiding humanity.

While we have lost the full picture of humanity's relationship to the angelic hierarchies over the many thousands of years, it is clear that the angels of God have continuously offered us guidance and protection. We are able to construct part of the picture from the simple stories handed down through generations. These stories sometimes were part of oral history; other times they were relayed by means of artistic images or written in sacred texts. Frequently we have ignored or misunderstood the correct nature of the warning they hold. We have also failed to heed the guidance given by the heavens.

We can grasp the seriousness of the present situation if we look back in ancient history, where events that occurred are reflected in the Bible and other texts. Certain leaders heeded the call from heaven. One such figure was Noah, who was instructed to build an ark to preserve plants, animal species, and human life in preparation for a great flood. Contrary to popular belief, this is not a myth but distant memory of an actual event that occurred—the destruction of an entire civilization. Misuse of spiritual powers, veneration of material security over spiritual development, and refusal to follow the guiding counsel of God created the factors that led to this destruction. Atlantis, an ancient continent which existed in the area that is now our Atlantic Ocean, was the place where this occurred. The North American and European continents did not exist as they do today. Although scholars such as Plato wrote about this lost continent, its existence has been denied by scientific materialists. Because something cannot be seen, measured, or touched does not mean that it does not exist. Current denial of Atlantis and its demise could be a way of avoiding the realization that humanity has already been responsible for total destruction of a civilization due to a series of negative choices. If we acknowledge this history, we are led to the realization that today we must awaken to the truth that we are once again facing planetary crises comparable to the sinking of Atlantis. *We must listen this time to the call of the angels of God.*

Some people are beginning to hear the call of heaven in their souls. This is the real reason for the popularity of angels as we approach the next century. Some people are beginning to sense, perhaps unconsciously, that our global civilization is undergoing tremendous changes, many of which are threatening to us physically, emotionally, and spiritually. We may have analyzed aspects of these changes. Still we fail to comprehend the threat which awaits us. We merely sense that life has become overwhelming and confusing. Our lives seem to flash by as technology and the demands of life become more complex. We even feel that time—and the speed with which events occur—is moving more rapidly. Thus a disparity exists for most people between spiritual beliefs and day-to-day survival in a world inundated with pressures, conflicts, violence, and continuous news reports of human suffering.

We are aware that an alarm has sounded. As birds and animals sense an impending natural disaster such as an earthquake, humans also sense that there is a crisis upon the horizon. We tell ourselves that the danger facing us is the breakdown of civilization due to natural or economic disasters. What we do not realize is that the imminent abyss *is of a spiritual nature that will have an impact on all of the manifest world.* It is of paramount interest to the angels of God that humanity not stumble into this abyss of darkness and suffering.

Humanity as a whole is shifting to a new level of consciousness which is effecting changes throughout our existence. The perception of angelic beings occurs so often now that it has become acceptable in our society to speak openly of such events. The awakening of spirituality is happening at the same time as the religions of the world are experiencing major challenges and as the veils are being lifted in the realm of personal perception. What usually would have been perceived only by initiates or spiritual leaders is now possible for everyone.

As the veils of understanding lift, a threshold appears. Humanity moves in consciousness not only as individuals but also as a group. *If we fail to cross this threshold of global spiritual consciousness because of our civilization's continued addiction to self and materialism we will fall into a great abyss filled with unimagined suffering.* As the veils of heaven are lifting we also feel the agonies of the underworld. Even those persons who hear the call of the angels will experience the suffering of others. *We are all one.* The spiritually advanced are always concerned with those who cannot maintain the path or who take detours because they have ignored the road signs of heaven.

If humanity learns to respond to the promptings of the angels of God rather than the agents of the underworld, we will make it across the threshold into a completely new level of consciousness filled with our most exquisite dreams of peace and love.

As a result of prayers and the good deeds of many people during the past century, the Creator has mercifully provided a safety barrier that may save us from falling into the abyss if we awaken and pay attention and if we believe that what is happening is real. *We need to become actively conscious of the angelic hierarchies which connect humanity and the Godhead in order to avoid the destruction of our civilization.* The angels of God are working as a group in a powerful way to awaken us before it is too late.

THE VIEW FROM HEAVEN

Through His angelic messengers, God is telling humanity that it is time to seek direct knowledge about the workings of the spiritual realms. This knowledge will assist each of us to become a better human being. The angels are not to be venerated. Learning about the hierarchies should expand our devotion to God. Making angels into idols is a major violation of spiritual law. Too often we forget that the angels have as a primary task helping humanity to transform with the use of *free will* into a civilization that reflects the highest spiritual qualities of the Divine.

One way of visualizing the importance of our making conscious choices with free will is to imagine guardian angels handing everyone a spiritual coloring book that has only the outlines of our destiny as willed by God. Each person can color it as he or she chooses, either with beautiful radiant colors or murky grays and black. Some persons may scribble all over the shapes with painful gestures in red. If a soul chooses to fill the outlines of destiny with gentle, harmonious colors, the angels provide better outlines with which to work. As abilities improve and the colors become more exquisite, the angel may even let the outlines be drawn freely.

Divine will comprises the specific decisions of our Creator. As we progress spiritually, the realization comes that if we align our decisions with those of God, we experience an expansion of freedom. However, if we are continually making decisions because of another person's influence, or without cognition, our decision to align our will with God's is meaningless. This is because there is no demonstration of higher thought. To just "obey" is not use of free will unless the individual has arrived at his or her own reason for selecting that particular path of obedience to the Divine as a way to learn humility.

Our Creator awaits the moment when each soul comes to an understanding that all love, all goodness and security, come from God. When the soul consciously *chooses* to love God in return, this is a special moment. It is even more significant when the soul realizes that God is the Source for all that is good, because then the will and the decisions of the Creator are preferred. Then the gift of free will has been used to its highest level. At such a moment the angels sing.

Each human, upon original creation, was provided with free will so that the opportunity for choice and experiences other than those of Divine perfection could occur and humanity could develop wisdom. Without such experience we, as souls, would be as the higher angelic ones resting in the radiance of God's love, knowing nothing else. Human beings have the opportunity to experience that which is not of God and reject it.

The point will eventually be reached when we

mature to the awareness that we have used our free will to select alignment with Godly force. It is at that time we exercise the gift of free will on the highest level. Following such a commitment, the words "Not my will, O God, but Thy will" take on major significance.

Since the angels of light work directly under the will of God, they serve to manifest Divine choices. In doing this, they can prompt, warn, and encourage us, but *never can they interfere in destiny as set by the Creator*. Therefore, the angels cannot circumvent our free will and demand that we do anything. They work hard to *encourage* humans to choose, of their own free will, to align with the Divine.

In order to consciously realign with the Creator out of love and wisdom, it was necessary for humanity to experience that which was opposed to God. To provide humanity with alternative choices while humans were developing as souls, members of the hierarchies who rebelled against God's will were permitted to interfere with human development—but only up to a point. When the situation threatens the relationship of souls to the Creator, the good angelic hierarchies intervene and encourage humans to free themselves from the influences of the rebellious ones. *This is what is happening today.* Those persons who refuse to reconnect with God will experience the abyss that we are approaching. This abyss will separate souls who are aligned to the light of God from the others. Such a separation occurs first on the inner planes and eventually leads to major planetary changes.

To avoid the abyss, we humans will find that help

from the angels is available if we seek to learn how the angels think and work. It is similar to developing any relationship. By sharing similar interests, two people will be drawn together and can communicate better. When we seek to understand our existence from the perspectives of the spiritual hierarchies, we have already begun to enter their realms through our thoughts. The more we can develop a sincere interest in sharing their work on behalf of God, the greater the opportunity for improvement in our individual and global destiny.

Working with angels does not mean that they become our ultimate authority. Only the Creator can be that. However, the rebellious angels of darkness have made successful attempts to rule humanity in ways that have led up to the current crisis we face. *It is time for us to awaken and free ourselves from powerful influences which have dulled our senses and led our global society to the brink of annihilation.*

There are increasing symptoms that our global society has succumbed to the influence of the forces of darkness. Some of these symptoms are:

- We entertain ourselves with displays of the lowest human traits, such as violence, sexual exhibitionism, desire for power, and ways to acquire more than we need of almost anything.

- Our society is becoming rapidly addicted to such poisons provided by the delinquent angels who are hoping to destroy our society by weakening our ability to refuse.

- We define success by the acquisition of power, money, or media coverage, rather than becoming an instrument of God.

- We accept the ugly, untrue, and morally depraved as normal, and we have ceased to react against the growing infatuation our society has with these areas in communications and the arts.

- We have begun to accept our relationships to animals and people as disposable options.

- We have separated justice in our legal system from spiritual truth.

- We have accepted as normal the violation of commitments.

- We venerate the form of the physical body rather than its purpose.

- We remove the elderly, poor, and infirm from our midst and abuse them.

- We are developing multiple family forms that confuse identity.

- We believe illness and hardships come to us from the outer world rather than being part of our own path of destiny.

- We have become a society of victims who blame others instead of actively working to transform life or situations.

- Immoral acts are accepted and publicized under a distorted view of free expression.

- Our society doubts true acts of selflessness while honoring the drive to acquire and use money or power.

- Our children have so little hope for the future that they end their lives or alter their destinies through rejection of spiritual knowledge.

- The treatment of criminal behavior is not designed to encourage moral transformation.

- There is a dangerous increase in viruses which cannot be treated or contained, creating a breakdown in social health.

- There is an increase in the number of spiritual charlatans that surpasses our ability to discern truth from illusion.

- There is an increase in violation of national ideals, such as the principle, in the United States, that one is presumed innocent until there is real proof of guilt.

- There is a decrease in the ability of people to feel a direct connection with God in their lives.

- We continue to fight over different views of God.

This is only a glimpse of a few of the large number of symptoms indicating crisis. Such conditions will continue to expand and to obstruct the angels of God, unless we begin purifying our individual lives. This will bring about angelic intervention that can start to reduce some of the terrible effects of the rebellious angels in our various societies.

To achieve personal transformation in our lives requires conscious initiative to change. This can only arise after identification of the problem, not through denial.

On the very highest level, it is true, there is only God and no opposition. However, in the manifested world we live in, we must confront these influences and then take action for their transformation. Of course the mightiest solution is to remember the ultimate power of God. Meanwhile, we can begin to work with our angel by recognizing areas of obstruction. Once we begin the identification process, the angels will surround us with help to overcome.

Chapter Two

THE TRUTH ABOUT ANGELS

CLARITY ON GUARDIAN ANGELS

One of the critical aspects of our time is that we can rarely tell truth from illusion. This stretches even into the subject of angels. There is much incorrect and incomplete information about guardian angels. For centuries there has been confusion and disagreement about the rankings of the spiritual hierarchies. Just because there are many books published in recent years on angels does not mean that true, or complete, information has been released. Part of the crisis our civilization faces is that there is a concerted effort on behalf of the angels of rebellion to provide misinformation in many beautiful packages. However, if one sincerely wishes to transform his or her soul while growing closer to the Creator, one's guardian angel will point out false information.

There are, however, some guideposts that an individual can follow to determine whether or not angels of God are providing the information. A shortcut test can be used. Whatever is received should strengthen your willingness to *honor God above all else in your life*. If the focus shifts to improving yourself for selfish purposes, or toward the acquisition of power in any form, or even to helping others for such hidden purposes as personal satisfaction and recognition, it cannot be coming from those beautiful radiant beings who love God more than we can comprehend. True offerings from heaven also come without force but with a free will option to reject anything given by the angels.

There are many current misconceptions about the angelic beings closest to humanity. The most frequent clarification needed is on the difference between actual angels and other beings, such as a deceased relative, who may be dwelling in the realms of heaven. Because they may be dwelling with angels, relatives who have died and appear in dreams or visions may have a similar angelic light or create the feeling of an angelic presence. But, alas, there is a great difference. The importance of clarifying this issue is that if we think about angels only in terms of deceased relatives or spirit guides, we are basically denying our guardian angel. Angels do not have the same type of free will that we humans do, and their focus is to help humanity develop toward the Divine. Also, the guardian angel assigned to you remains with you continuously, whereas humans who have entered the spiritual realms through death have other stages of spiritual development awaiting them. They may periodically bless a family with a presence and, perhaps, radiate the light of heaven. Eventually, their guardian angel will lead them onward after death toward higher spheres and away from earth consciousness.

A term often used for personalities that do not have a physical body, but may inspire and sometimes provide knowledge, is "spirit guides." These are very different from angels because they once lived as humans. Since they also have other tasks to accomplish throughout creation, they are available to a person only periodically. They can inspire for positive or negative purposes, according to their own spiritual growth.

Negative guides are attracted by thoughts, feelings, and actions that are out of alignment with the will of God. Spirit guides have much more of a human attitude and are quite directive and specific in any knowledge relayed. Angels, however, are bound by God's law of free will for all humans. A good way to determine the difference between real angelic presences and spirit guides, who can often be purveyors of illusion, is that angels offer potentials and do not give orders. Instead they relay guidance from the Divine that is permissible within the situation.

The guardian is far more than just a protector of life or a companion through the veils before birth and after death when we return to spiritual heights. *What the angel guards most of all is memory of your purpose.* The complexity of soul development is such that memory of existence prior to birth must be dimmed in most cases to enable improved consciousness to arise from free will choices. The guardian angel is a caretaker throughout time for the potential of your soul.

Another area of confusion about guardian angels has to do with their appearance and whether they ever have human bodies. The reason for this mix-up has a lot to do with lack of awareness about the types of energy fields or spiritual bodies. For example, the human is actually only halfway along in its development. We operate with three vehicles or bodies of energy, led by a fourth, and sometimes we have flashes of the three additional potentials for our spiritual growth (see chapter four for further discussion of these topics).

Angels have different bodies than humans. They do not covet having a human body as has been suggested in certain films and works of art. Only delinquent angels, fallen ones, lust after the human form.

The reason for this is that guardian angels have as their densest vehicle the etheric body of radiant light. For them to seek the human physical form would be to go backward. They have already concluded an earlier stage in their own growth when they experienced much the same type of development as humans but without the physical body we humans have today.

This means that angels operate on higher levels of energy than humans. They access spiritual forces that enable them to appear in different forms. If you can only picture your guardian angel in a business suit with a briefcase, that is how your angel will appear to you. *How an angel reveals itself has to do with the human's level of consciousness.*

In their normal state, angels are beings of heavenly light who can be seen with energy fields around them that can have a shape similar to wings. The wings are only an *indication* of the many dimensions in which the guardian angel is active.

It is because of the etheric body and its flowing, life-maintaining nature that guardian angels are connected to water in the natural world and, in particular, where water and air combine. This is why images of angels often appear in the clouds. Viewing clouds is one way to understand the body in which an angel dwells.

You may ask: what about all the reports of angels who look like human beings? If they are angels of God, their physical appearance would be for the benefit of one or more humans. Thus the angel would allow itself to be seen in a way that would be acceptable to the human's belief structure. You can be assured, though, that if the being who appeared to one was an angel of God, any physical body would not be real. The angel might seem to have flesh but it would not be as dense as ours. This is also the reason that angels are known to disappear so quickly. An angel can easily disperse the image of a physical body instantaneously and return to its normal body of light.

It is difficult for most people to see the etheric form of an angel, but the skill can be developed as the viewer progresses spiritually. It is far more important to respond to the guidance of the angel rather than to see one. Many people can sense the presence of their guardian angel. They report that a feeling of lightness and peace seems to surround them. So often we may feel this and not realize that our angel may be the source.

Most of us know that even with all the gifts of

the angel, we are still not to venerate this being in any way. Acknowledgment is fine. Veneration should be saved *for God alone*. I want to share an image that will better explain this relationship. Envision the spiritual hierarchies as a large corporation with the Creator as the head. Orders for action flow out of the head office to the divisions, to the regions, to the departments, to the front office reception center. Your guardian angel is very much like the reception and communication (mailroom) center. Even though the angel has all sorts of advanced abilities and knowledge, it is aware of the limited role of the receptionist and refers everything to a supervisor. The angelic supervisors over the guardian angels are the archangels. When you pray to God, the angel receives this prayer and passes it on. The guardian angel would like to be spoken to, or thought of, but not prayed to directly. Praying directly to a guardian angel would be exactly like expecting the receptionist to act like the owner of the company.

The question arises if it is even necessary to give your angel a name. I recommend that we not limit our angel in this way. Our interest should only begin with the desire to identify this being of goodness. The path to a successful relationship is not to be concerned about names or to try to see what your own angel looks like. It is much more important to learn to *respond* to the guiding impulse of your angel.

It is valuable to realize that there are some areas of your life where the angel has specific authority. These areas have to do with changes in your destiny. The guardian angel is responsible for leading you to other souls and experiences that will ultimately transform or expand your consciousness *so that it becomes completely in alignment with God while still being filled with the uniqueness of your identity.*

Perhaps you could say that, prior to your birth, you and your guardian angel had conferences with even more influential angelic beings, and a general outline of events, limitations, and potentials was created for the present life. The human soul can fill in the outline of life with darkness or perhaps use creative impulses and moral determination to complete the outline in the most beautiful radiant colors. The choice of what one does within the outline is left up to the human being. Now let's suppose that someone creates exquisite colors in the outline, perhaps sooner than expected and possibly indicative of great love for the Creator. The angel might respond that the choices of the human have been better than expected, so there was need for a revised and improved outline, perhaps with more room for use of potentials.

What you do each day truly creates an effect on your future potentials and those connections and experiences toward which the guardian angel can lead. If you resist life events or respond negatively, it is as if you were to refuse to fill in the outline. Sadly, you will make little progress.

With the popularity of angel stories during the past decade, a question frequently arises for people who have not felt or seen their angel. They wonder if they have one or if they have to do something to have an angel with them. Such questions arise because they have not been exposed to the knowledge of how angels work and the responsibilities assigned to them.

Your guardian angel is _always_ with you; thus, there is no need to "connect" or act in a certain way to make your angel come to you. The two of you are connected in consciousness from the moment of your heavenly creation. What you may be experiencing is only loss of spiritual memory. You just forgot your angel, but it has always been there. The more you remember and focus your consciousness in the same direction as the angel's, the more you will find the angel interactive in your life.

It is the heavenly responsibility of the guardian angel to guide you toward relationships with all the types of people that you agreed to meet prior to your birth. Sometimes there is an indebtedness, a kindness that has to be repaid, or perhaps a new perspective on the other person is needed. It could be an opportunity to accept a kindness or to stop repeating an old pattern. Whatever the purpose, the guardian angel will work within time and space in your life to connect you with the other human being to set up the potentials for spiritual growth that are within the relationship.

If you look at your connections with other people in this way, you will begin to recognize the imprint of the guardian angel in your life. If there are any spiritual lessons that have not been completed by you, those types of individuals will continue to be presented into your life as an opportunity for growth. _We must remember that whatever our guardian angel leads us toward, even if it may be uncomfortable due to our limited consciousness at the time, it is healthy for the development of our spirit._

One helpful point in terms of relationships is to remember that we need to discern whether the association has entered our life as a result of the prompting of the guardian, or as a result of our own negative patterns or thoughts that can attract toxic relationships. Once the association that might be toxic is brought into conscious thought in terms of the angels and there is a willingness to improve oneself, the guardian angel can assist in healing the situation.

When the subject of relationships comes up, it leads to thoughts of love. One area we fail to understand in terms of the spiritual hierarchies is that they are highly advanced in knowledge of love. They are experts in comparison to humanity. Each person's guardian angel serves God and watches over its human with such immense love that we cannot comprehend it. They love with no expectation of recognition let alone gratitude for all they do. They are sustained out of the central force of love that emanates from the Creator down through each hierarchy until it reaches humanity by means of the guardian angel.

There are moments in our lives when we experience a sort of ecstasy, as when we feel that another human being loves us, or when we feel our own heart filled with this emotion. This is the merest, tiniest reflection of what the guardian angel feels for you. The angel has the responsibility to relay to you directly the love of God, *if you will receive it*. Because many of us refuse to receive it directly, the angels have to work with the guardian angels of other people so that through another person they can bring this love into our lives.

Angels, then, make it possible for humanity to love. We need only remember that any relationship upon which we depend for little droplets of love is only a replica of the real relationship with God. Even though humanity has developed a detached view of the Creator's ability or willingness to love us directly and to connect with us on a personal basis, the angels are now working to expand human awareness about the truth of this situation. Such an expansion of perception will change our choices and actions for the better.

So the question follows: what has happened to the people who don't feel any love in their lives? The answer is that they have not chosen or believed in the love of God for them personally. If you don't believe that there is a source for love, it is difficult to experience love as real. Usually the experience is filled with illusions, selfishness, fear of loss, and pain. When we let go of the ownership of love, then the angels can release the Creator's love force directly into our lives.

Another area we do not always understand about guardian angels is that these beings are connected to God's wisdom, otherwise known as the Holy Spirit, or, in some traditions, the Divine Feminine. There is a deep relationship between the Divine Feminine and the angels which has much to do with the reason Isis, Sophia, and Mary, mother of Jesus, all have connections with the angels. In addition, there is an ancient mystery about the need for wisdom to lead the way to the experience of love.

This means that the angel has access to great wisdom. Many people realize knowledge can be accel-

erated by prayer. The guardian angel has greater understanding than the human and has the ability to provide
wisdom, or in some cases genius, if it will be for the
betterment of soul development. This is often the secret of unique talent. The wisdom of God has truly
inspired the individual through his or her guardian
angel.

CLARITY ON LIFE'S MYSTERIES

Each night during sleep our guardian angel helps us review what we have done with the outline of potentials. This is extremely important because what we do
during the waking hours determines the levels we can
reach during sleep.

It works this way: There are nine levels of angelic
beings which progressively have more spiritual light.
When we go to sleep, it is the responsibility of the
guardian angel to escort us to the realms of heaven. If
we have filled our thinking with positive images during the day, then, at night, we have sufficient light in
our souls to enter the spiritual world. If, however, our
thoughts, feelings, and perhaps actions are connected
to negativity and reflect a denial of God, we are only
able to enter limited realms during sleep. These realms
have very little spiritual light. Therefore, the angel has
difficulty in accompanying us because the angel is
filled with great light. Whenever the angel is forced to
be around negative thinking, it feels the way a human
does when walking into a room without sufficient
oxygen.

It is very much our own choice whether we will experience nightmares during sleep or images of heavenly bliss. To be sure, the more one experiences a loftier level of sleep, the better will be the next day's life events, which can be taken back into sleep, leading eventually to transformation on all levels.

In special situations, the sleeper can be lifted to experience the presence of an important religious figure. Such experiences can never be demanded but are given to the individual when inspiration or clarity is needed. Sometimes this can include the angel itself becoming visible to the human.

It is with the care of our guardian angel that we experience not only sleep but also entry into life (as well as entrance back into the spiritual world at death). The timing of birth is very important, as are the parents one chooses. The specific circumstances for spiritual development are selected with the help of the guardian angel as well as members of the other hierarchies. The guardian angel maintains the memory of the purpose for each life choice and the potentials provided with each.

At our birth into this world, the angel works very closely with us. Although we may have other angels involved in our lives, the guardian angel is responsible for the process of helping the soul develop and finally enter the new little body. Just prior to birth the soul of the baby is prompted by the guardian angel to view an outline of the lifetime ahead. This will be the last view of the reasons for many life experiences until death (or unless revealed by the guardian angel during the life). In most cases a veil of unconsciousness descends that obscures the memory of pre-birth. However, because the last viewing of the life ahead happens just prior to birth, this is one of the reasons why infants after arriving need to be soothed and comforted as well as warmed and nourished. It is especially effective for the parents to speak directly to the newborn and promise to help him or her through the difficulties of life. Hold the image that it is an experienced soul you address; the body is only that which is brand new and so vulnerable.

It is difficult to explain the full range of activity of the guardian angels and the other hierarchies without explaining a little about life before birth and after death. Despite the many distortions on the subject of reincarnation, due largely to organized religion, there are elements of truth to consider. It takes more than one lifetime to reach spiritual perfection. This does not mean, however, that humans reincarnate as rocks or as animals, as is often thought in certain Eastern philosophies. This would be regressive. Humans only dwell in the human body.

Prior to birth there is an opportunity for us to select life situations that will benefit spiritual growth. It is up to us whether we use or misuse the situations life presents us. The guardian angel is there throughout and is available to clarify and remind us of the reason for the circumstances in which we have chosen to live. Many of these reasons have much to do with the successful or unsuccessful response to potentials during a previous lifetime.

The purpose of the death process is basically the same as that of sleep; it is an opportunity to rest and be nourished directly by the realms of heaven. If our lives are not filled with the kind of positive thinking during the daytime that will lead to this experience each time we sleep, then we experience a sort of deprivation at night. Remember, *the guardian angel can only accompany us to levels of consciousness that maintain the Light of God.* The more an individual has filled his or her mind, heart, and actions with a spiritual perspective during life, the greater the experience of nurturance and rest after death.

The subject of multiple lifetimes can be soothing when one realizes that the design encourages moral development arising from freedom. Each time on earth has within it potentials for the person to make better choices in thinking, feeling, and actions. This can lead to an increase in faith and love of God.

Such an understanding provides a viewpoint of the guardian angel that is very important. The angel has accompanied your soul throughout all previous experiences up to the present. No one other than the Creator knows you better or has more belief in your goodness and potentials. The guardian angel cannot interfere with your choices. Thus, when a decision is made or behavior continued that can have a negative impact on your spiritual growth, the angel experiences a sadness.

There are religions that consider the subject of multiple lifetimes heretical. This is understandable given that the facts are often distorted. For instance, many people do not know that early Christian believers accepted sequential life experiences as a natural process. It was only a few centuries after the crucifixion of Jesus Christ that church doctrine was *changed* so that the knowledge about reincarnation was banned. Church leaders believed that if people were conscious of the workings of heaven while they were alive and took personal responsibility for their lives rather than placing it on an outside authority, religion could not expand.

It is really difficult to progress toward the spiritual world without clarity on the important relationships we form with the kingdoms of nature that are connected to the angels, or without understanding specific connections with different angel hierarchies.

These elemental beings in the realm of nature are very important for our existence. They are the caretakers of the mineral and plant kingdoms as well as workers with earth, air, fire, and water. We live surrounded by them even if we cannot perceive their presence. The elementals in the realm of nature are quite sensitive to the thoughts that stream from humanity. Even if we live in a city, there are elementals active with earth, air, fire, and water wherever we go. When we give off negative thoughts, it upsets the elementals, which is one of the reasons we are experiencing such powerful earthquakes, hurricanes, floods, fires, and other earth traumas.

 There *is* something that we can do. Be conscious of the presence of elementals, and wherever you go, whether in a park or at the ocean, in an airplane or entering a building, realize that the angels have been active in the form of their workers, the elementals. Appreciation of the activity of these beings combined with holding the image of God wherever one walks or moves on this planet creates a positive effect.

Eventually, the nature forces will respond in a positive way and there might be an exquisite sunset, a gentle breeze that is beyond description, or a feeling that the earth beneath us greets us wherever we walk. Such an awareness will also help the work of the angelic beings who oversee the whole planet and will naturally contribute to the activity of the archangels. However, all of this can occur *only* if it is based on a sincere love of God.

What can be done to develop a true closeness with the hierarchies? We can develop a sense of sincere wonder at the creation of all that exists in the physical universe. Appreciation of the genius of our functioning world will open one to the deeper levels of wisdom about the spiritual realms. It is very much like having a composer for a friend. When you express truthful appreciation for his music, chances are great that the composer will privately share special music he has written. This same principle applies throughout the hierarchies. The more we show sincere recognition and gratitude for what they have created through their allegiance to God, the more these angelic beings will reveal to us.

Chapter Three

A SPIRITUAL WHO'S WHO

HUMANITY

Humanity is God's most treasured creation. We have the power to elevate the world through the use of free will. To understand the relationship between humanity and the hierarchies, we must examine the threefold nature of humans: physical, etheric, and astral.

Throughout the past millennium, the church has distorted this knowledge. Much of this misunderstanding arose in A.D. 869 during a special gathering of church leaders, the fourth Council of Constantinople. At the end of the nineteenth century, Dr. Rudolf Steiner provided a shocking picture of the effects of this meeting on the Christianity of that time. According to Dr. Steiner, those church leaders agreed to declare officially that humanity was no longer composed of three parts—a body, a soul, and a spirit—but was only twofold. The decree stated that humans had only a body and a soul. The spirit would be maintained through the church. This expanded the dependence of human beings on church authority through the centuries. Similar changes have occurred in other religions to strengthen a particular viewpoint. Knowledge of the threefold human is essential today as a prerequisite for conscious work with the angels of God. To do this work means developing greater self-responsibility and determination to respond to life more fully. *Our civilization needs every person to awaken.*

We all know the first part, the body, which is the densest. It is a magnificent symphony of angelic creation blended into its current form by all the hierarchies under the will of God. Our physical body is very much connected to the mineral kingdom. This can be observed when the other parts of the human leave the body at death. The remains then become like stone.

There must be another force field that helps our lungs to breathe, blood to flow, health to radiate. This second part is called the etheric body, and is connected to the plant kingdom. We cannot grow, nor be healed, nor be alive without the etheric body. It is composed of light, is somewhat transparent, and can glow. When we die it takes three days for this force field to disperse into the etheric force field that surrounds the earth. When a relative appears to a loved one during these three days, the radiance seen is actually the light of the etheric body. Appearances after three days are frequently more symbolic or are for the purpose of direct comfort and communication. It is also possible for us to be in contact with the soul of a deceased relative in our sleep, but only with the blessings of the guardian angels.

A third force field exists. It is larger than the physical body and encompasses it. You experience it every time you dream and find yourself running in a beautiful field or doing something physical. You are using a completely different force field, your astral body.

When death occurs the angel lifts everything away from the physical body. This includes the etheric life forces and the astral sheath composed of emotions of attraction and repulsion of the Ego. This spirit, or "egg," is the most wonderful part of all, and it should be viewed as our eternal identity.

When the etheric body disperses into the etheric force field of the earth, a process which takes three days, the remaining Ego is still surrounded by the astral sheath for a considerable time. This usually is comparable to the amount of sleep time spent during the lifetime. So, for example, if a person lives to be ninety, approximately thirty years earth time will be necessary to complete the dispersion of the astral forces and their return to the astral plane surrounding the earth. This time period is when the soul voluntarily relinquishes all negativity in feeling before entering the presence of higher angelic beings.

THE HIERARCHIES

The recent expansion—on a global scale—of interest in the subject of angels has puzzled many, including sociologists and the media. The public's sincere involvement with the subject is frequently explained as an occurrence orchestrated by mass-marketing interests or due to the fractionation of our lives leading into realms of fancy. These are limited and inaccurate explanations for both the surging impulse to connect with angels and the magnitude of angelic experiences reported.

An important element in understanding this resurging interest in angels has to do with the relationship of the spiritual beings we call guardian angels to the other members of the spiritual hierarchies.

We might remember that the subject of angels is far more complex than just becoming aware of one's own guardian angel. When a person understands that guardian angels are only one of nine levels (known as choirs) of angelic beings, it also becomes clear that impulses from the will of God are actually transferred from the highest spiritual hierarchy, the seraphim, through the various choirs until received by individual guardian angels. Therefore, any global awakening has been created by the will of God.

During the last century in Europe, an extraordinary spiritual initiate, Dr. Rudolf Steiner (1861–1925), founder of the doctrine anthroposophy, worked to provide considerable amounts of personal research information on this vast subject. Dr. Steiner could consciously work with the spiritual hierarchies as well as explain their functions and responsibilities. He spent a lifetime teaching how to develop the human soul in a balanced way that would enable one to enter heavenly dimensions while fully conscious.

An important clarification made by Dr. Steiner involved a prerequisite for working with angels. He said we need to develop new organs of perception that could enable us to experience beyond the capacity of the physical brain. These organs of perception will be developed by all of us as we progress morally. Through his skill in using these organs of purified imagination, inspiration, and intuition, he was able to provide vast amounts of material on spiritual topics, especially the workings of the angelic hierarchies. In addition to his own research, he was a scholar of classical angelology, cosmology, the natural sciences, philosophy, history, physiology, and architecture. Upon his death in 1925 he had established major impulses in childhood education (today there are Waldorf Schools all over the world), medicine, art, biblical studies, agriculture, and much more. He was known for his deep devotion to the Christ Being, and he felt that clear knowledge about the activity of Archangel Michael was essential for our time.

The nine choirs, as described by Dr. Steiner, are as follows:

First Hierarchy
    Seraphim
    Cherubim
    Thrones
Second Hierarchy
    Kyriotetes
    Dynameis
    Exousiai

THIRD HIERARCHY
    Archai
    Archangels
    Angeloi—Guardian Angels*

This ranking is also recognized in classical angel treatises, such as the *Summa Theologica* of Thomas Aquinas and *The Celestial Hierarchy* of Dionysius the Areopagite. Dr. Steiner gave new names to the members of the hierarchies to reflect that they were "spirits" of God. He explained, in depth, the role each choir of angelic beings plays in the development of human consciousness.

ANGELS, ARCHANGELS, AND ARCHAI

If we realize that the guardian angels who accompany humanity throughout existence are very much concerned with the relationships between people as well as with maintaining individual contact between each soul and the Divine, we have a valid starting point for understanding the realm of the archangels.

For thousands of years, scholars and theologians have argued over the names of the major seven archangels. The emphasis in the study of these beings has been on the individual archangels rather than the responsibilities and activities of that particular realm.

---

*All guardian angels are angeloi, but not all angeloi are acting as guardians.

Even in the arts, depiction of these spiritual beings has been connected to biblical references rather than to their cosmic task.

The seven most prominent archangels, as confirmed by Dr. Rudolf Steiner, are as follows: Raphael, Uriel, Gabriel, Michael, Zadkiel, Samiel, and Oriphael. The most active ones at this time are the first four beings, with whom humanity is most familiar, and I will discuss these four in more detail later.

Each of the archangels has a connection to specific times of the year, otherwise known as seasons. The year is divided into four quadrants in which one can feel the influence of individual archangels. Because the position of the planet to the sun causes opposite seasons at the northern and southern hemispheres, two of the four main archangels always work in conjunction with one another: Michael and Raphael, Gabriel and Uriel.

The activities of the archangels are as follows:

Northern Hemisphere	Archangel	Southern Hemisphere	Archangel
Summer	Uriel	Winter	Gabriel
Autumn	Michael	Spring	Raphael
Winter	Gabriel	Summer	Uriel
Spring	Raphael	Autumn	Michael

Each archangel works in harmony with the other archangel whose influence can be felt in the opposite hemisphere during a specific season. These influences do not have to do with weather but with how the archangels actually work with human consciousness.

To obtain a proper view of the archangels as part of the universal plan, let us remember that they are responsible for *groups* of human souls, such as various cultures, tribes, nations, or other groupings wherever people live together. (If one accepts the idea of multiple lifetimes, then it becomes clear that having a selection of cultural or national experiences in different parts of the earth is beneficial for a person's spiritual development.) The archangels aligned to the will of God are in harmony even if the humans of their particular cultures or nations have different religions. *It is only humanity that argues over religion, not angels.* Be aware that the delinquent angels want to instill the impulse of conflict over the subject of the Divine even within a specific religion.

One way to view the relationships between guardian angels and archangels is to imagine the archangel as an immediate supervisor over your angel. Any work or service you might do that involves the culture where you live or to which you might seek to contribute must be directed through to the archangel of that region or culture. When your own angel is able to relay to the archangel the purity of your intentions combined with sincere willingness to serve in harmony, then help will be forthcoming from the archangels. *The question one should ask is how to purify the intentions.* The best helper in this cleansing process is the guardian angel, who will respond if asked.

The archangels are very much involved with languages because of their work in the development of different cultures. To know this interest of the archangels is to realize a very important point. One cannot abuse language and reach the archangels. The problem is not only in using abusive words, as in swearing, but also has even more to do with excessive words as well as distortion, or not using words in a truthful fashion. Superficial talk is painful for the archangels. However, they are particularly pleased when humanity uses sounds, or words, to express spiritual truth.

The archangels do not communicate in the same manner as our guardian angel. Their interest is in the contributions we are willing to make toward the society, culture, or nation in which we live. Although this can strengthen love for the country where we reside, it does not mean nationalistic pride, which *repels* the archangels. National pride can arouse a feeling of superiority. Positive thought on the purpose behind each culture, with genuine appreciation of those cultures that are different from our own, is needed.

Carefully monitoring our speech is a most effective way to connect with the realm of the archangels. Release sounds from your mouth that praise the Divine and this will please the archangels. Remember, swearing and excessive use of words (chitchat) are experienced as uncomfortable by the archangels. Likewise, any words used to communicate should reflect the truth.

Very few individuals actually work with a particular archangel even though they may feel a personal connection. We must always remember that when working with angels there are seductions for the lower human ego that come disguised in the highest ideals. It is a misconception that you can dial up an archangel as if you were dialing a friend on the telephone.

Discernment between truth and illusion is needed every moment. The reason people feel a strong link with one archangel has to do with the existence of "schools" in the spiritual realm in which souls are prepared for tasks on earth under the guidance of specific archangels.

This century, in particular, people feel they have a personal connection to Archangel Michael. The School of Archangel Michael was extremely active in preparing souls for current times. Frequently, a person may feel that the Archangel Michael is his or her own guardian angel when the usual case is that the guardian angel assigned is part of the School of Michael. I will explain more about this school later in the chapter. Angels that have sworn allegiance to Michael frequently bear the same name but are not of the rank of archangels.

Persons who feel a connection with Gabriel, Raphael, or Uriel have also been prepared before this life.

Wherever one is located on the earth, the guardian angel will work in harmony with the archangelic hierarchy of that region for major world events.

Archangel Gabriel

The Archangel Gabriel is a specialist in communication. The focus of Gabriel is always on the words we use, the ideas we seek to transmit, and the degree of truth present.

Gabriel, known for his role in the Annunciation, is often depicted holding a trumpet, which symbolizes

God's power to help humanity vibrate at a higher level. New creative spiritual impulses can flow to humanity through the archangels to the guardian angels to humanity. Gabriel plays a very important role in this process, sounding the tones from heaven that can transform even the densest of matter to insights, inspiration, and Divine intuition.

Gabriel, along with the Divine Feminine, is also strongly linked with human birth processes. When any culture or nation is about to enter a major change, whether through revelation or the birth of special beings who can act as leading influences, Gabriel's consciousness is active. Presently we are experiencing the birth of a new consciousness on a global level. This is being assisted in a variety of ways by the activities of Gabriel. One activity involves the increasing reports of people actually seeing their guardian angel. Another involves the numerous incidents in this century when specific messages have been given from the being known as Mary, mother of Jesus Christ.

Gabriel's role in this planetary awakening is to direct individual guardian angels to work with their human charges during sleep. Gabriel has an interest in our sleep life and our capacity to dream because many revelations occur during this time. This explains why people all over the world report that they did not have any particular interest in angels and then awoke one morning with a sudden intense determination to explore the subject. Their interest seems to expand and deepen with each book read. These individuals also report an overwhelming desire to discover some way to help the world. They have started to respond to the message relayed from heaven to humanity by their own guardian angel during sleep.

The overall purpose of this modern annunciation process that humanity is undergoing has to do with the Divine Feminine. We have the potential to let the spiritual feminine impulses, which are deeply connected to the wisdom of the universe, give birth to completely new levels of consciousness for cultures all over the world. This can mean we will be able to enter the realms of heaven during our waking times as well as during sleep, provided we are able to recognize the spiritual hierarchies that make up the realms of heaven. Such a process would involve the development of a new type of thinking.

Gabriel is not only connected with the birth of human souls but also works to prepare us for much of the activity of the Archangel Michael, which is explained later in this section. Because Gabriel's influence is experienced in the northern hemisphere during the winter while Uriel's is felt in the southern hemisphere during their summer, there is a balance between these archangels. The season of Gabriel means a time when it is easier for the heavens to communicate with humanity. If you think about this, you will realize that wintertime is the appropriate season to do deep inner work, to read spiritual books, to expand commitments to God. Gabriel has had many festivals that occur during his season in the northern hemisphere—such as Christmas, Hanukkah, and holy days in other religions.

The connection with Uriel means that while one side of the globe is experiencing a deepening of spiritual communication and awareness of the angelic realms, people in the opposite hemisphere are being taught truth. Uriel strips away all that is false and maintains an almost stern focus on humanity to encourage us to manifest inner world ideals into the outer world. The tendency of Uriel is to expose everything, just as we humans do during the summertime by wearing lighter clothing when the northern hemisphere is under the influence of this powerful archangel.

Gabriel, therefore, has a specific task in awakening humanity. It is being fulfilled with the help of Archangel Uriel, who is the great teacher and revealer of truth.

Archangel Raphael

Biblical texts portray this celestial being in a limited fashion. Most of the references relate to the connection between this archangel and healing—for example, the story of Tobias and the help of Raphael. In this account Raphael travels disguised with Tobias, the son of Tobit who was blind. The archangel does not let Tobias know who he is until the journey has ended. He teaches Tobias, who has caught a fish, how to use each part of the creature, including the heart, liver, and gall, as a medicine to heal his father's eyes.

On the inner planes, Raphael is the great balancer. It is through this ability to provide balance throughout time that he is known to heal. Originally the symbol of Raphael was the staff with two serpents, one white and one black, intertwined in an upward fashion. This symbol refers to the "open secret" of all healing—the balancing of light and darkness in our souls and in our bodies. It is interesting to note that over the years, the American Medical Association removed the aspect of balance by leaving only one serpent on the staff of healing.

Raphael has another important area of influence: he is involved with boundaries where two realms meet, such as the horizon where what is above meets that which is below. Sunsets as well as sunrises are occasions where night and day meet. Subconsciously, when we approach sunrise or sunset, we are aware of an extraordinary balance taking place in the outer light and this stimulates an inner balance to occur. This is the explanation for why many creative persons, depending on their own nature, will experience a rush of ideas at sunrise or sunset. It is also the reason why many illnesses, such as fevers, will change for the better or worse at these times of day.

To begin to understand the influence of Raphael we need to see the connection he has to the seasons and to the other archangel with whom he shares planetary influence, Michael. While Raphael is being felt in the northern hemisphere during the springtime, Michael is being experienced in the southern hemisphere as it undergoes autumn. This cooperation appears again when Raphael becomes the seasonal influence during springtime in the southern hemisphere, while Michael's presence is being felt during autumn in the northern hemisphere.

The impact of Michael, as archangel, has a great deal to do with his connection during this century to the realm of the archai, which I will describe later in this chapter. The aspect of Michael that is important in conjunction with Raphael has to do with spiritual courage.

If we think of Raphael as working to help us create a balance for our world, then it becomes clear that this will be attained through the quality of spiritual courage. Whether we are speaking of healing or balance on physical, mental, or emotional levels, courage is necessary for the process. Conversely, true spiritual courage arises out of the desire to create true balance in a given situation.

This also holds true in the realm of the arts. Raphael is known to stimulate art forms which honor the Divine. True creativity that originates from the light of God requires an inner balance between truth, beauty, and goodness. To achieve this, there is a need for spiritual courage rather than egotism.

All the archangels work with the development of culture and, therefore, are active with such creative people as artists, musicians, writers, and performers. Raphael's influence to heal a cultural situation, however, is blocked by any creative person's pride in his or her own genius. Similarly, the guardian angel is unable to receive impulses from the archangel in terms of nations or larger groups of people where there is an emotion similar to national pride, and a connection then develops with the rebellious archangels. Love of one's nation is essential; it is *pride* which leads to aggression or the domination of others. This blocks the workings of the archangels and prevents Raphael from working to transform darkness.

Sometimes the problem is not knowing what would provide balance. This is because of our limited perspective. Our own guardian angels will always offer love, comfort, and hope to us as individual souls. However, the archangels will establish balance in ways that may be puzzling from our perspective. The balance of power between one nation or culture and another has not occurred by accident, but comes from a long history. The archangels are able to view things from higher up on the mountain and can remember the past better than we do and can see farther into the future.

Raphael brings healing to a culture or nation by stimulating its people to serve the greater purposes of humanity. If we can begin to see history from the viewpoint of the necessary rise and decline of cultures which provide different soul experiences for humanity, we will understand balance from the viewpoint of Archangel Raphael.

Archangel Michael

Among the archangels, the being known as Michael holds a special place. One reason is that when we experienced the period of manifestation known as Ancient Sun, long before our solar system was created, Michael was the most advanced. It was at this time he took a specific initiative, which explains why he is so beloved by the Creator. When certain delinquent beings began to cause havoc in the realms of heaven by staging a general rebellion, Michael defended God's plan for human development. He spoke in defense of the Creator and encouraged other angelic beings to acknowledge their allegiance to God. Those beings who did not state their fidelity fell under the influence of Lucifer. This is one of the first confrontations between Michael and Lucifer. Periodically Archangel Michael limits the areas of influence of these delinquent angels.

This act of Michael's courage is on a level that we can barely imagine. It is another commitment from Archangel Michael that any human being who seeks his protection from the influences of darkness shall have it. All one needs to do is call for his help. But, be prepared. To remove negative influences may also require some inner transformation for yourself, so I always advise people to be willing to accept whatever Archangel Michael does to protect their relationship with God. He will rescue a person from difficulty only if there is an effort by that soul to overcome the dragon within his or her own thinking, feeling, or action. Without this willingness to transform self, one would just be using this great archangel, which is certainly a very unwise thing to do. He is a protector of only those who love God and will not be manipulated.

The season of Michael in the northern hemisphere is autumn, a time when we evaluate our harvest and prepare for winter. During this same season we have the influence of Raphael in the southern hemisphere seeking to bring balance as a path toward healing. We must realize that both archangels are concerned with overcoming darkness by establishing light. However, Michael's way is different from Raphael's. Michael brings light through the human mind, through consciousness, that has the quality of inner freedom. One of the ways to discern the illusions of the delinquent angels is that their influence is binding, enslaving on an increasing scale. One of the ways to discern whether you are receiving true communication or guidance from your own angels is if you see evidence that there is harmony and consistency between the two. For example, the freedom recognizable as the trademark of Archangel Michael is supported by all other hierarchies of God.

Autumn is a wonderful time of year to remove the dead leaves in your life and to prepare for the greater spiritual focus that occurs during winter and the holy season. As you release useless thoughts and feelings that hinder your path, purify your thinking and deeds so that angels will want to come close to you during the winter and bring inspiration. Be conscious of our connection to nature's death process. Use this time to reflect on those areas of your consciousness that are not yet free and begin to work on them. It is also a wonderful opportunity to connect with Archangel Michael by deepening your commitment to the Divine. Picture the sort of being he must be to stand before the rebellious angels and defend God. The question may come to us: do we personally defend God sufficiently in our own lives? By focusing on such thoughts, you will begin to understand what motivates this remarkable archangel.

Archangel Uriel

The reputation of this powerful archangel has been somewhat stern. There is a lot of misinformation about his actual duties as archangel. He is not the angel of death and destruction. Instead, he is the great teacher, who strips away the nonessentials and reveals whatever is hidden. He leads humanity to truthfulness to match the outer manifestation with the inner. In this way, *it becomes clear that if one is not aligned to the Divine, Uriel's influence can be experienced as painful.* If, however, the individual and the culture or society strive toward a purity of expression both inwardly and outwardly, Uriel will reveal the loving teacher he is. Wondrous things about the spiritual world not normally available become accessible. Clarity comes to issues that were confused and directions into a healthy future are shown.

Uriel works in conjunction with Archangel Gabriel on a seasonal basis. When Uriel is active during the northern hemisphere's summer, Gabriel's influence can be felt in the southern hemisphere during winter. To understand the effect this has on the world, we must realize that we have the combined influences of Uriel and Gabriel seeking a new level of consciousness through revelation among humanity that will be inwardly purified and ready to accept Divine word. Gabriel's activity of revelation or annunciation cannot occur without inner preparation.

Uriel and the United States

The implication of this joint relationship between Uriel and Gabriel has significance for one particular nation in the world—the United States of America. Due to the different cultures among the people of our country, on the archangel level we operated very much on a committee basis prior to recent years. Some of the impulses of the good archangelic beings clashed with the interests of the rebellious ones.

I have become aware of a major event that occurred in the late 1980s *that has nothing to do with any politics.* As a result of many prayers and the awakening of numerous souls within the United States, the spiritual hierarchies placed Uriel in the position of archangel over our country. Since that time, nothing remains hidden. People are experiencing the demanding gaze of Uriel testing us to determine the quality of our inner nature. That which is polluted in our thinking and our deeds has been made quite obvious. Uriel is active in purifying our nation in ways we can barely imagine. He, also, is working with the impulse of Michael to bring contrasts of light versus darkness in our lives *so we can make a choice.*

Uriel has the responsibility of leading our nation to a level of truth and action where we can become forerunners in a new Michaelic consciousness. Much of this activity has to do with the positive impulses that led to the formation of our nation. Though many people do not understand its significance, the guiding force toward independence, the signature of Archangel Michael, had much to do with the need for inner freedom in thought. *Uriel is working to reawaken that original impulse so our nation can fulfill its purpose.*

The Archai

Once you understand the role of the archangels in the development of cultures and nations, it becomes easier to comprehend the next level, the realm of the archai.

These angelic beings are overseers of the planetary civilization as a whole. It is their perspective to see far into the past and way ahead into the future. What we consider tragic, perhaps, in the decline of a civilization may be necessary from the view of the archai. Likewise, they also take into account the buildup of civilizations.

As a guardian angel might focus on the length of a human life, and an archangel observe the birth and death of nations and specific cultures ranging over hundreds of years, the archai realm concentrates on thousands of years of earth history as civilization rises and declines.

What is it that the archai are trying to develop? They are seeking to provide different experiences throughout time for souls that are born. If our planetary civilization remained the same, there would be no opportunity for growth.

The current head of the realm of the archai is none other than the great Archangel Michael. Dr. Rudolf Steiner explained that in the last third of the nineteenth century a very important change occurred, and that change is still influencing our civilization at present. This is a sort of changing of the guard among the archai.

In order to create different planetary conditions,

each of seven archangels is allowed to oversee humanity for a period of 350 years. They have rotated responsibilities in the position of chief archai for many thousands of years. In 1879 Archangel Michael became the reigning archai, taking over from Archangel Gabriel.

The significance of this event will become clearer if we remember that Archangel Michael is the one who did battle with the rebellious forces and defended heaven's plan for humanity to express inner freedom through the development of a spiritualized thinking process. Since Michael became archai, our civilization has taken remarkable steps to establish a contrast between materialism and the desire for spiritual growth not linked to scientific proof. It is as if the planetary family can feel the lines being drawn, and we must select our priorities.

The position of Archangel Michael as leading archai at the present time also means that we are experiencing many inner battles on all levels with the forces of rebellion. Spiritual courage, which is offered by Michael, is needed as never before.

The pathway through this difficult time is to become conscious of the spiritual world and knowledgeable about the workings of the angelic realms. Such awareness will instill a thirst for inner freedom and develop capacities for avoiding illusion. It is very much a Michaelic command to the archangels and to the guardian angels to awaken humanity before the current battle is lost. *Those who do not heed the warnings about realigning priorities in our consciousness will find them-*

selves awakening too late. The time is NOW, and the goal is inner freedom connected to a conscious knowledge of the spiritual world.

Archangel Michael is encouraging humanity to go beyond faith, to develop *inner resources and new ways of thinking that will lead to direct experience of the higher worlds.* Once an individual has a conscious connection with the realms of heaven, it is possible for him or her to become a living reserve of God's love and wisdom. When this happens, harmony is possible on the global level that will avert major disasters whether due to forces of nature or the hand of humans.

The gift of Michael, as archai, is the ability that humanity now has to develop self in a new way, through use of spiritual imagination, inspiration, and intuition, which is the activity of *becoming the truth oneself.* Imagination is really "I can visualize"; inspiration is "I interact"; and intuition is "I am one."

EXOUSIAI, DYNAMEIS, AND KYRIOTETES

Above the archai there are three realms of spiritual beings. Closest to the archai are the exousiai, followed by the dynameis, with the kyriotetes farthest from humanity and closest to the thrones. There is confusion and actual disagreement in the classical literature about the role of this central threefold hierarchy, but one consistency is the relationship it has to the operating sphere of the sun. This is the reason why so many ancient cultures venerated sun beings. They were consciously aware of the existence of these beings.

One of the other names for the exousiai is the *elohim.* I think the name Dr. Rudolf Steiner gave to this hierarchy, *spirits of form,* provides a clarity about their role and leads us away from the confusion of ancient documents. These angelic beings are the protectors and developers of prototypes for all that exists in our cosmos.

Spirits of motion is another name for the dynameis. Names by which you may recognize them from biblical sources are "mights," or "virtues."

The mystery behind the dynameis is shown in their name. They are the overseers of dynamic energy in our solar system and in our lives. On the smallest scale, they help us move inwardly, seeking to encourage us away from lethargy in daily living. On the larger scale they are responsible, on behalf of God, for keeping the planets in motion. Without the specific impulses of the dynameis, there would be no growth and no development. If we remember that the exousiai shape the forms or archetypes for existence, it becomes clear that there is a necessary relationship with the dynameis who can activate those shapes or forms necessary for Divine expression.

Another name for the next realm of the angelic hierarchies, the kyriotetes, also provides a good explanation for their activity. They have been called *spirits of wisdom* by Dr. Steiner. In ancient texts they have been referred to as dominions. Their sphere of activity, along with the exousiai and the dynameis, is connected to our sun.

To arrive at an understanding of the purposes of the kyriotetes, there is a need for some explanation about the connection between wisdom and the Divine Feminine. All true wisdom emanates from the God Center but flows from the Divine Feminine aspect of God. Some connect this to the Holy Spirit. This part of the Godhead was involved in the development of the universe in terms of the tasks assigned to the angelic hierarchies. Sometimes there is much deeper knowledge behind surface knowledge. Such is the case with the recognition of the being known as Mary, mother of Jesus Christ, as connected with angels. She has been called Queen of Angels by the Catholic Church. There is a substantial truth behind this, but it refers to the Divine force that works through the being known as Mary, as well as through other figures such as Isis, Sophia, and Eve. Another secret about kyriotetes is that "kyrio" means "Lord."

Through realizing the connection between the spirits of wisdom, or kyriotetes, and the Divine Feminine, it is possible to explain another unique aspect of this rank of angels. This realm of angels is particularly close to Jesus Christ before and after His lifetime on earth. Wherever one experiences the healthy impulse of wisdom, there should be a connection with the spiritual force of love. And where there is real cosmic Love, then Wisdom has been active in its development.

Thrones, Cherubim, and Seraphim

The very closeness of this threefold group of spiritual beings to the Godhead, or Trinity, makes it essential to provide an overview of the interactions in ascending order of responsibility: thrones, cherubim, and, closest to the Creator, the seraphim.

It is important for us to envision the tremendous level of sacrifice that is the sustaining influence of the thrones. *Any idea or thought that leads to manifestation by the will of God exists because these beings gave out from their own spiritual bodies their own essence as energy for manifestation.* This is the deeper reason for their name of thrones, because they do sustain and support the Godhead.

One of the ways to learn about the thrones, or even to gain their attention, is through a conscious refusal of any power other than that of God. These beings are living embodiments of Divine power, but they sacrifice all desire for power in preference to total devotion to God. The thrones, or *spirits of will*, however, take particular interest in human activity originating from selfless service. One cannot maintain any real connection with the thrones without having shown a similar ability to give out his or her own essence in service to God as was done by this hierarchy.

The task of the thrones is to fulfill Divine will by creating, through actions of consciousness, a bridge between God and manifestation. To achieve this requires sacrifices from these beings beyond what we can comprehend while in physical form. These beings establish space for creation through sacrifice.

The thrones have been an area of confusion in angelology because some sources believe this rank is closest to the Godhead. There are biblical references to the *throne of God*, and other images of their connection to wheels in certain documents. Perhaps clarity can come if we realize the actual meaning of a throne is a chair which holds a royal being. A chair of this sort is still an image that refers to the ability to hold, to provide necessary foundation to hold the impulses of the Divine. The wheels have to do with the symbol of movement, combined with the thought of circular motion, which is another way of saying, *the thrones work in maintaining eternity*.

The desire to learn about angels is a serious concern to the thrones, who seek to encourage humans to become willing participants in creation *by learning to give of self in service to the will of God*.

The cherubim are not little baby angels with wings. That image also is a distortion of a real truth. The cherubim maintain an extraordinary amount of purity and innocence, and so they are symbolically portrayed in the form of a winged child. If we continue to trivialize these remarkable beings, we miss the truth.

The task of the cherubim is to receive the thoughts of God as relayed to them from the seraphim and then "ponder" over them. Another way of looking at their contribution is to think of their pondering as both an endorsement and a germination time before actual manifestation that occurs with the help of the thrones.

The correct inner name of the seraphim is *spirits of love*. In this hierarchy closest to God, the love of the seraphim is on a much purer level than how one human being can love another. The kind of love the seraphim hold is total and beyond our comprehension. It is their task to receive into this field of love the thoughts and images of God. This ability to receive these thoughts and images is created out of the highest form of sacrifice. They basically give up their essence to *surround and protect the thoughts of God*. Nothing exists in our universe without a Divine thought. The seraphim protect these thoughts through the perfection of their love.

This is a wonderful point at which to explain why it is so very hard for humanity to love at anywhere near the level that comes from the guardian angels, let alone the seraphim. This is because *humans expect to receive something back when loving another*, whether it is only a smile or a positive experience. We are almost totally unable to love only for the heavenly intent of manifesting God through individual sacrifice. Because we are not willing or not able to love in such a completely unrestricted and generous way, there is very little love coming from humans. Much of the love we do experience through our relationships is relayed to us from the angels. Original love is very difficult for humans, perhaps because unconsciously it is known to be the only force that has no return and that transcends the laws of cause and effect. When a parent loves a child or a mate, this feeling is beneficial to the world and to one's own life. It has the potential of paying off spiritual debts; therefore, a return is experienced even if not consciously. The kind of love we need to develop is on such a level that the direction is only outward like the rays of the sun.

A CREATION STORY

To provide you with just an inkling of the vastness of our relationship to the spiritual hierarchies and the history of our world that predates the establishment of time, I will tell you a story. Behind this tale is a great truth. Because of our limited three-dimensional mind, it is easier for us to receive complex cosmic knowledge in the form of simplified images. Our ancestors knew this, and much of the basis of this story has been passed down in folktales of various cultures, each with different words or details but with remarkable similarity.

> *Once, long, long ago before time, our God decided to experience a new level of consciousness. He separated out part of Himself to create an energy field from which to manifest Himself. This became the force of Consciousness, or Wisdom. The first activity was the creation of the Word, an aspect of Himself that would maintain the fabric of existence through the force of Love. God remained the source of Will. The angelic*

hierarchies, from the seraphim to the angeloi, were created from the substance of the God-head.

A moment occurred when the first stage of creation of our cosmos actually began. There arose an energy similar to but not exactly the same as heat. During this event the thrones were very active, establishing the foundation of our universe. This occurrence is given the name Ancient Saturn, which has only a distant connection to the planet of the same name.

After this first expression of Divine consciousness in the form of heat, there was a return to the Source—a period of cosmic sleep in which there was no manifestation.

Then the next phase began with a repeat of the heat expression, followed by a further development. The heat began to glow, to radiate. Air was involved in the process. This became the earliest stage of what we now know in our current solar system as the light from the sun; thus that period of Divine expression is called the Ancient Sun Period. In our story, we still do not have our current solar system or the development of the human body as we know it.

Once again there was a cosmic sleep, a time of rest. This was followed by another repetition of the earlier stages—heat, then radiance, and eventually the new expression manifested in the form of movement of light. The name for this stage, too, has nothing to do with the current planet of the same name. It is called the Ancient Moon Period.

After another cosmic sleep and re-capitulation of earlier stages, this energy expression progressed further and finally developed into the solar system that we currently have for the purpose of developing human consciousness. The thrones set the operating principle for our whole solar system by taking a specific action. They gave up substance from their own bodies of energy to provide for the manifestation of our solar system and the development of the human form. In this case, the name of the period has very much to do with the planet on which we dwell, Earth. Our experience here is called the Fourth Round and was well known among the ancients.

The hopeful news is that there is a heavenly archetype for three more stages of development long after our Earth stage is completed, making a total of seven. The last three are given the names on the inner planes of Jupiter, Venus, and Vulcan, and each period will involve the formation of an entirely new solar system.

There is a reason for you to know the perspective of our evolution from the cosmic view. Each one of those periods created the foundation for what would become the human being. During the first stage, Ancient Saturn, the seed impulse was created for what was to become the physical body and, in terms of spiritual realms, the ancient origin of the mineral kingdom. The Ancient Sun Period provided the seed force for what would become the life energy body of the human being and also the origin of the plant kingdom. The Ancient Moon Period developed the archetype for the third force field that surrounds our physical form, otherwise referred to as the astral body. The origins of the animal kingdom also developed during the Ancient Moon Period.

You may already have guessed that the present stage of existence, Earth, has to do with the development of the human being, the apex of which is the awakening of spiritual consciousness.

The importance of knowing this immense panorama of creation is that you will understand more clearly when I say that the angelic hierarchies directly contributed to this development that was initiated out of the will of God. At each stage, specific members of the hierarchy directly above humanity reached levels of their own perfection. During this present manifestation, they are working to lead us away from a potential disaster that is of our own doing. Despite spiritual blessings and actual interventions in the past, we are at a point where what we do in the next few years will determine the destiny of all of humanity as well as the angelic hierarchies and the various kingdoms of nature.

With the completion of each of these evolutionary periods, the beings composing the ranks of the spiritual hierarchies advanced in consciousness consistent with the amount of sacrifice demonstrated. The more they offered their essence for the development of what would become humanity at the Earth stage, the more they personally evolved. This could only happen if they were in harmony with the will of God.

THE SECRET OF DARKNESS

As with any situation of group evolution, there were angelic beings who held themselves back and refused to participate fully in spiritual development. At the end of each major stage and prior to the cosmic rest, these delinquent beings were isolated so that they would not interfere with future development. These beings compose the many ranks of rebellious angels who consistently attempt to interfere with the spiritual evolution of humanity. If one becomes aware of how ancient these rebellious forces are, one realizes the tremendous effect of such beings on humanity.

The good news is that periodically a containment policy goes into effect to balance everything. The image of the Archangel Michael slaying the dragon (often represented as the armor-clad St. George doing battle with the beast) reflects an actual truth. As a highly advanced being during the time of the Sun stage, this Archangel took the initiative to defend the heavenly spheres against the ravaging energies of the delinquent ones symbolized by the dragon. He was loyal to the Creator's intention in the development of humanity and caused there to be a sorting in the heavens. This resulted in the actual removal of delinquent beings from heavenly realms. However, those beings were permitted to tempt and seduce individual humanity at various stages. What is little realized is that this battle between the dragon image of rebellious forces and the angels of God led by the Archangel Michael happens over and over, as long as we have manifestation in physical form.

It is because of the possibility of personal error due to influences from rebellious forces that the Creator assigned an angel to each human being to accompany him or her throughout existence both in the spiritual world and on earth. This being of the spiritual hierarchies is from the rank of angeloi closest to humanity. One of its many tasks is to protect from the influences that will corrupt, with one stipulation: *the human must have developed soul faculties that honor the Divine or a willingness to attain a closer connection to God* for the angel to be fully active. If the human has responded to the seduction of the adversary forces, the angel is still assigned the soul. However, the level of intervention in that human's destiny is severely limited until a change in consciousness is evident.

It is a sensible idea to discern the influence of rebellious angels in our lives so that we can deactivate their effects. The major striving of these fallen angels is in three major directions depending on the origin of the particular rebellious influence.

One seductive force, which has historically been referred to as Lucifer, originated from the realm of kyriotetes before becoming active in the realms of the archangels. Because of biblical sources, most of us think of only one rebellious angel known as Lucifer. In fact there are *three* deadly resistance forces to the will of God. The second one is connected to the rebellious exousiai, the spirits of form. The third force has its origin in the realm of the rebellious dynameis. This third force, the azuras, are just beginning to have an impact on our world and can be felt in such situations as mass murders accomplished without any emotion.

The rebellious or delinquent exousiai operate through a being given the name Ahriman in ancient Persian texts. These negative beings impel us to hold on to forms longer than it was designed by God. An example of their influence on humanity has to do with people retaining outdated thinking which has become solidified and rigid. This causes hardening of consciousness as well as a refusal to look into the spiritual world. There is usually a tremendous amount of fear and condemnation that prohibits any spiritual growth.

Another example of this negative influence is the use of numbers in our society to determine who a person is, whether this refers to the amount of money they have, the pervasive use of a series of numbers to identify the person, or the expanding use of computer data to develop backgrounds on people. This divides humanity and provides a totally false reality about who the person is and even about the nature of the society. Numbers cannot be the basis for our consciousness.

Ahriman's goal is to derail humanity's spiritual growth by misuse of heavenly forms and to prevent growth by instilling fear and greed. The many addictions our society has in relation to forms has led to the materialistic society in which we live.

The effect of Ahriman also appears with the veneration of objects that represent angels, rather than venerating God. And it has to do with any work involving angels where money has become more important than service to others.

A very subtle but destructive influence of these rebellious forces is felt when people seek to put spiritual realities into a material format that places the emphasis on the phenomena of an event rather than on spiritual truths being communicated. This might include some television programs where the emphasis has been on rescues by angels. The stories are all important; the problem is that people can easily dismiss the subject of angels because of veneration of angelic paraphernalia such as are sold in the growing number of angel stores. They may also question why they personally don't have a guardian angel in their life to perform dramatic rescues similar to the ones portrayed on a Hollywood movie set.

One last example of the influences of rebellious spirits of form on our lives has to do with the desire to manipulate angels to acquire what we think we need. This happens in very subtle ways that one can innocently stumble into out of a sincere desire to connect with one's guardian angel. What I refer to is the growing number of "easy access codes" to working with angels. These have nothing to do with personal inner transformation or developing a closer relationship to God. One of the indicators to look for is whether any source places more emphasis on the form, rules, or recipes for action *rather than a focus on God*.

I have sometimes described the misuse of form in terms of angels by clarifying that one should not, for example, light three candles and whistle for an angel. This behavior creates only illusions because of the intention to command angels through form. The emphasis should be on God, not the angels. Neither God nor his angelic ones should be treated like servants to be beckoned through the power of form, or ritual. This is why ritual magic of *all types* is connected to the underworld.

Whenever a person overcomes the negative use of form, Ahriman is not happy. He does not like humanity's striving to bring itself closer to the heavenly realms in ways that prevent the solidification process that signals success by the rebellious angels.

The good news is that these influences can be offset and in many instances transformed by our consciousness and how we view things. If we begin to accept that we are no more than our social security number or other numeric identifier, this delusion becomes real. Instead, every time we use such a number we should remember our relationship to God and that we will never be only a number to our Creator. If we maintain this larger perspective, we will return to seeing other persons—and treating them—as carriers of Divine presence.

Whenever we are facing the effects of these rebellious ones, fear is stimulated, and a strong desire comes over us to refuse to change. We retreat into a rocklike part of our thinking that does not really protect us at all but leads to all sorts of other problems like condemning others who have different views from our own. Such confrontations become the basis of wars on many levels.

There is no greater power to dissolve the rigid influence of these delinquent spirits of form than to be loving. The warmth of sincere love which honors God above all else melts the resistance. We may all have experienced the cold, numbers-only thinking of clerks serving the public, when before our eyes they blossom into smiling, gracious human beings who will overcome the "rules" (or misshapen forms) through their own initiative, as long as we first saw the potential for Divine presence in their eyes.

Most important in developing an awareness of the rebellious exousiai or spirits of form is to realize that God is the architect for all that is truly meant to exist. That which is a useless form, or inappropriate, or damaging to the human spirit, we can change. The change comes only when we replace the negative form with a higher one filled with impulses from the heavens.

The most effective way to create spiritual images that are beneficial to our inner life is to expand the activity of faith. When fear is present, faith has been given second place. I have often said that *fear is the greatest eraser of God's potentials.* The rebellious forces win the battle easily through simple paralysis. Without expansion of faith and belief in God as more essential than anything else, the fears grow and grow until darkness sets in. Whenever we truly rely on faith, especially when we don't see any guarantee or proof (a frequent request from the rebellious forces), then the blessings of the good exousiai can enter our lives.

When the rebellious dynameis influence our lives, it can lead to a disruption of motion in all we do. The impulse can be for us to experience things sped up at a tremendous rate, which has happened to many of us, especially during the past few years. The motions within our own lives, let alone on the planetary level, have become so fast that we are nearly out of control.

One example of this speed is in the field of communications. Not long ago in terms of earth history it would be necessary to wait weeks, perhaps months, and sometimes years for an exchange of letters. We moved forward to telegraph, then telephone with written letters to follow. The 1980s brought the possibility for guaranteed overnight delivery of a letter, a rapid improvement over the pony express system that was in use a hundred years ago. Now we have fax machines, and computers that create instant messages. Instant communication seems so appealing. But is it really? Has it not diminished the time for response to almost nothing? On a spiritual level, this has effectively sped up time for us individually and also as a society. Damage may well be done to our inner spiritual resources in a multitude of ways—the most serious perhaps being that we have become a nation demanding to know everything instantaneously, with this demand blocking the blessing impulses of the angels. We need to begin to think in *angel time* rather than allow ourselves to be whirling in useless motion under the urging of negative dynameis.

The solution to this intrusive influence is to consciously connect all motions we make in our lives with the quality of balance. At the same time, all motions created should be for the purpose of strengthening and releasing into such actions truth, beauty, and goodness. If one does this, then the effects of the positive dynameis in life will be to establish balance and order rather than chaos.

The angelic beings who are responsible for keeping order in our solar system in terms of energies will also provide for personal order in one's life physically, mentally, and spiritually.

The delinquent kyriotetes created an interference which is a little more serious. Because the Christ Being and Divine wisdom are connected to the kyriotetes who operate in harmony with God's will, the rebellious being, Lucifer, consciously distorts the combination of wisdom and light. He seeks to seduce humanity into a distorted view of their own abilities in the form of egotism wrapped in seductive packages of truth, beauty, and goodness. These are the very same qualities that the spirits of wisdom seek to instill in humanity in balance and without deformity. One way to determine the difference between good and rebellious spirits of wisdom is that the influence of the negative forces makes one seek a beautiful realm away from the earth so appealing that one would forgo spiritual destiny and walk away from helping other humans.

Further indication of the interference from forces

opposing the good kyriotetes is that they seduce one further into the self, leading to egotism and in its final stages to insanity. This is very dangerous in terms of an awareness of angels, because it is in the interest of these delinquent forces to entice humans away from their lives through such means as the belief that they themselves are angels rather than human souls. This effect is serious because such delusion leads the human to forgo destined experiences, thus causing difficulty for the guardian angel.

You can be sure that if any angel of God appears in the flesh, it would be for only a momentary experience and not for a lifetime. Yes, people can *work with* angels and learn to behave like them. Any being born out of flesh who claims to actually be an angel and not a member of humanity may well be under the influence of the negative angels. At this time it is the desire of rebellious angels to incarnate in human form. It is the work of the angels of God to inspire, help, and uplift humanity through encouragement of free will used in the highest fashion. For an angel of God to completely become flesh would mean that an angel would accept a body on a level of existence that was backward. This does not mean, however, that angels can not and have not worked cooperatively with humans. This is done all the time. An angel knows its purpose, and the human being remembers that he or she is a human even when working with the angels of God and accessing those realms.

The key realization is that these outer negative battles reflect a major conflict in the spiritual world that really escalated between 1840 and 1879 in astral spheres surrounding the earth. There had been other major conflicts in the heavens before the nineteenth century, and each time Archangel Michael worked in direct opposition to the defiant angels who sought to interfere with the will of God.

When Lucifer rebelled, Michael removed this influence from the heavens and cast the whole operation down to the earth plane. This was one of the many achievements that have given Michael a favored status in the heavens. How does this containment policy, repeated periodically, affect humanity? It provides us with *choice*. It is always Michael's hope that we will continuously reject such influences leading to egotism, withdrawal, and delusional thinking.

The adversary forces knew that a major change in planetary authority among the angelic hierarchies was about to take place during the last third of the nineteenth century. The position of global spirit, or chief archai, was about to rotate once again. Among the many archangels seven of them share stretches of leadership in this position, each lasting about 350 years. Uriel and Zadkiel do not participate in this way but have other responsibilities. Since the time of Christ, when Oriphael was the archai, there were successive rulerships by Anael, Zachariel, Raphael, and lastly Gabriel from the mid-1500s to 1879. Michael's last rulership as archai was before Oriphael's, in preparation for the Judeo-Christian era. At that point, Greek civilization flourished with great scholars such as Socrates, Plato, and Aristotle. Gabriel, who was the reigning archai up until 1879, had an effect on civilization by encouraging the development of natural science, which is still having an impact on us today. This heavenly gift was intended to be part of humanity's spiritual education in learning about the forces of nature, but the impulses were seized by the adversaries and have led to our current attachment to materialism. Natural science was supposed to have brought humanity closer to God rather than intensify the feeling of separation. Toward the end of Gabriel's reign, the Archangel Michael began to prepare for his 350 years of leadership and found himself once more having to contain an influence.

During the last century, however, the forces Michael had to confront in the realms of heaven were not Luciferic in origin but went by another name, Ahrimanic. These impulses sought to wrest from humanity the proper uses of material existence and thus prevent the mission of Michael, which had been in preparation since the time of Christ. Michael was to bring to humanity, to allow to stream through his consciousness to ours, the knowledge of the spiritual worlds. This knowledge is given to those beings who make a decision to align themselves with God. The critical threat to the adversary forces was that if humanity received knowledge about the heavens and the truth about illusions and how the rebellious forces actually work, human souls might well refuse to aid them any longer.

Starting in 1840 for a period of about thirty-nine years, Archangel Michael entered into a major conflict with the Ahrimanic powers. The battle occurred in the astral realm of heaven and was felt by those who were sensitive or who had higher sight. The wars that began on the physical plane during the twentieth century are directly connected to this spiritual battle.

Most of us are unaware of the extent to which the heavens and earth are connected. When humanity fights among itself, it hinders the work of heaven; when the realms of heaven experience opposition, this is reflected later on earth.

The conflict in the spiritual world reached a culmination in 1879 when Archangel Michael finally succeeded in containing the rebellious influences of Ahriman. Michael then became the current archai, Spirit of Our Age, overseer of our civilization.

The School of Michael

When Archangel Michael was preparing for this elevated position and was aware of the extent of damage which had been done to the heavenly gift of Gabriel in terms of natural science and understanding of the human body, there was an important gathering called. Those angels who in earlier battles had helped Michael in the containment of the rebellious one, Lucifer, as well as those angels who supported God in the current battle with Ahriman, gathered in the heavens. Human souls who were committed to God and the angels of light who were preparing to be born in the twentieth century also attended. There was specific training given in preparation for the new battle ahead which would take place among humanity on earth rather than in the realms of heaven. Each human soul becomes the new battlefield with both types of adversaries, Luciferic and Ahrimanic, striving to lure humanity away from its heavenly potential.

The preparations for this battle were given in the spiritual world under the name of the School of Michael. Many angels came, as well as human souls in spiritual form. They learned that someday a call would go forth from the highest angelic beings to which they would respond. At the heavenly school, teachings included cosmic history, the works of the hierarchies, and the intentions of Michael to free humanity in the realm of thinking. *If humans could be encouraged to develop the ability to think freely, they would find a way to transform their actions as well as balance the emotional parts of their lives.*

We are now in the second hundred years of Michael's reign and his influence can be felt. Decisions are to be made everywhere. Contrasts appear all over the world between mental enslavement and free will cognitive processes. It has now been pointed out that a threat awaits humanity if natural science is to be used to construct the world's conception of the future. This, sadly, is already under development. Other contrasts exist between such a material perspective as "We are what we eat," wherein substance is viewed as having more power than consciousness, versus learning that the true source of nourishment connected to the spiritual life transcends the limits of the body.

People are also becoming interested in angels in a very strong way, because, as archai, Michael inspires the other archangels, who infuse the guardian angels with impulses to encourage thoughts about the heavens. Many of the souls who have recently become interested in angels so quickly and intensely are souls who were prepared before birth in the School of Michael.

Ahriman seeks actively to prevent humanity from opening the door to heaven. There are two major ways in which his forces operate successfully. One is to encourage rigid thinking that will reject true spiritual knowledge out of fear that it opposes a particular religious view. Michael, who is known to work so very closely with the Christ Being, seeks to inspire open choice in religious paths. The second way Ahriman encourages humanity to keep the doors to heaven closed is to create confusion. Wherever there is confusion, people will make poor choices or place themselves under the will of another. The world of spiritual knowledge is filled with contradictions and illusions as never before. There are instant experts on the subject of angels who have no real inner knowledge of the workings of the universe or who do not demonstrate any long-term experience working consciously with higher beings. *The confusion about truth makes it possible for Ahriman to interest souls in gaining knowledge about angels, not to be of service but for personal power or financial gain.* As soon as this is done, direct experience with the true angels of God is prevented. That is why it is so critical that one's motives be examined periodically and all acts of selflessness encouraged daily.

Confusion has truly made its entrance into the field of angelology, particularly in the last ten years. Sincere interest in the subject of angels and significant events in personal lives led people to venture into the often conflicting realm of angel literature, angel lectures, and an increasing fog about who really knows the truth or what is valid. This confusion designed by the angelic underworld is proving successful. People are fixing their gaze where Ahriman wants, not where Michael would prefer. Ahriman would like to have people focus (even to the point of veneration) on the materialization of angels, including physical objects in the shape of angels, as well as on learning about the heavens while not mentioning the Creator. Michael encourages spiritual commitments to be translated into deeds that can then be received by him into the spiritual world for purposes that will help humanity. Ahriman does not like it when souls awaken to the call of heaven by devoting their inner life to God. He would rather people venerate the angels who work for God.

It is an understatement to say that *the heavens are knocking at our door*. True messengers of God are encouraging us to open the doors of our conscious mind. At the same time we are being bombarded with invitations to open our souls to rebellious forces frequently offering security in materialism and greed. Sadly, some members of humanity have chosen the latter because they mistakenly thought that the battle was being won by Ahriman, and they wanted to share in the spoils of war.

As we discussed in chapter two, these battles with the dragons will keep happening until we make a conscious decision to devote all our energies toward aligning ourselves with God. If we do not open the door to the right influences, we will not only have to deal with the current dragon of Ahriman's influence, but also another dragon will join him. Such an effect is beginning to show itself in the types of killings where a person annihilates a group of strangers for no special reason other than to experience the process of killing. There is a lack of any sense of morality. Souls of such individuals have become deadened by the bonds of materialism.

One of the most important images to keep in mind is the image of Michael, the archangel, in a position of conquest. He is wielding a sword of iron that represents the courage available within the heart of every person. When we wield a sword of truth that emanates from the heart, it vanquishes the opposition. Michael has repeatedly overcome darkness by the light of truth.

Chapter Four

TRANSFORMING
YOUR LIFE

On the very day I began this chapter in which I intended to bring you to an understanding of how the angels can transform our lives, I found a monarch butterfly's wing on my living room floor. This was during the middle of winter on the East Coast of the United States. After the initial impact of the heavenly gift, I realized the angels were letting me know their truth could come across the threshold of words and be received. If it was possible to manifest a butterfly wing at so perfect a time, they would help in building a relationship between you, the reader, and me as we look into this important subject. Maybe the process of transformation symbolized by the butterfly will become a true experience as I share these ideas with you.

As I mentioned in chapter one, our world is in serious trouble. *There is no more time left for us to ignore the need to take action in our personal lives and expand our contributions to society wherever we live on this planet.* Greater inner responsibility is a basic requirement for change and part of the process in working with the angels.

Our ability to respond to life situations with an enlightened perspective, which is the goal our guardian angels are leading us toward, is hampered by barriers we have constructed out of our free will.

These barriers can be overcome by the angel but not without the permission of the human in its charge. This is to protect the right of each person to express free choice even if the choice is a negative one.

However, it is essential that we pay some attention to the barriers we have accidentally or willfully constructed to interfere with our heavenly connections. When we decide to remove these barriers and release our angel to greater freedom in our lives, transformation actually happens.

To begin our journey through transformation, we need to look at how to create sufficient purity in our souls to permit the angels to work unhindered on a group level and as individuals. A first step is to identify areas of life where we are under the influence of the rebellious angelic forces. By examining some of the symptoms that indicate a conscious or unconscious relationship to these forces, we begin our journey on the path to freedom from the bonds of the rebellious angels.

Each person has his or her own personal list that is known deep in the soul. While you read this chapter, it is a good idea to write yours out on paper, provided further action is taken and the list itself doesn't become an obstacle. In general, areas of difficulty where we obstruct the angels of God can be divided into three categories: thoughts, feelings, and actions.

The first area can have the most negative effect on the relationships to angels because our thoughts often affect our feelings, which in turn color the actions that result from both.

We should view ourselves as threefold beings, with one area of our body, the nervous system, connected to the thinking process; another area, the lungs, related to the feeling part of ourselves; and a third area, designated as the will system, directly tied to the limbs and metabolic processes. These three areas are not independent of one another. It is helpful, however, to evaluate spiritual obstacles in these three categories.

THOUGHTS

Some of the symptoms that indicate your thinking has been influenced by the rebellious angels are listed for your reflection. As you read them, think of any others that need to be examined. It is only by first identifying the symptoms that we can start the transformation process.

- negative thoughts that deny the presence, help, or love of God

- dishonest thinking that leads to illusions about oneself and others

- inability to develop original thoughts

- willingness to accept, without challenge, thoughts from the group mind

- self-deception regarding the future—such as believing that one will win the lottery

- thinking that it is perfectly acceptable to cheat others and justifying it by saying that "everyone does it"

- lack of discernment that leads to misinformation

- ideas that the only way to succeed is to compete with others rather than one's own goals

- judgment that condemns others, rather than healthy discernment for the purpose of choice

- lack of healthy imaginative thinking

- lack of ability to discipline thoughts

I find it is a good idea to periodically do an evaluation of my thoughts. I do it objectively as if I were an angel who had the ability to look deep into my mind. When you try this exercise you should seek to recognize areas of darkness as well as areas of particularly brilliant light. Then try to figure out how you can use the bright thoughts to illuminate and transform the darker thoughts. It works. Try it. You will find that the angels are very interested in such efforts and will provide a lot of assistance.

Many of us have allowed our brains to become very lazy. We are dependent on having ideas spoon-fed to us by the media and entertainment industry without the need to truly reflect at all on what has been presented. How often do we actually challenge ideas or do research at the library on topics of interest and apply the knowledge? How many times do we come across a difficult poem, a passage in literature or non-fiction that is not clear, and stay with it until we comprehend it? How many times have we created an original thought?

The reason for this brain paralysis that comes upon us from time to time is that we have not yet spiritualized our thinking. Our religious teachers have emphasized the importance of purified thought, yet we continue to accept prepackaged ideas of goodness as replacements for the prepackaged ideas given to us by rebellious angels. Rarely do we create original thoughts. To do this requires improving the way we think as well as the quality of the thoughts themselves.

How can we do this? One of the best ways to start is to begin to trace the origins of each idea you develop. Question where it came from. Did it arise from sense perception? Did the thought seem to come to you from nowhere? Is it attached to a memory or experience of some sort?

If you can develop the habit of running an identification check on the origins of your thoughts, some wonderful results will follow. First, you will become aware of the tiny amount of original thinking which you do. With this reflection will come the awareness of a connection between inner freedom and original thought. Second, the process of discovering how to develop this new type of free thinking will become an important focus in your life. When you hear someone else's ideas, you will wonder where they originated. Eventually, you will be able to sense or perceive if such thinking is the product of the goodness of the individual working creatively or whether the rebellious angels have stimulated the ideas.

Our world of thought is produced by us either in freedom under the loving guidance of the forces of good or under the direct imprisoning manipulation of delinquent angelic beings who use human thinking to achieve their destructive goals.

This negative influence rarely leads to the extreme case of bad spirits dwelling in human minds, which is known as "being possessed." Rather, I am referring to how we have become so lazy that we unconsciously fall under the subtle influence of rebellious angels affecting our decisions. *It happens because we have not trained ourselves to think freely.*

When our thoughts are not filled with sufficient light, it becomes almost painful for the angels to guide us. We create sort of a toxic cloud around us that pollutes not only the earthly dimension but the etheric world as well.

We are dwellers in a minimum of three spheres of consciousness: the physical, the etheric, and the astral. The first, the physical, is greatly affected by the second, the etheric. When we sleep, it is the activity of the angels to strengthen and heal the physical body by activating the etheric forces to repair and reenliven it. This is why we feel refreshed after sleep. However, we lso awaken without feeling very renewed. This is caused by our thoughts obstructing the angels in their work.

Our thinking process involves not only the brain but also these etheric forces. Did you ever notice that it was difficult to think when you were ill or tired? The etheric forces that surround and interpenetrate the physical body are very responsive to our thoughts. Our memories are also imprinted on these energy fields. If we build positive memories and thoughts that reflect Divine truth, it becomes possible for our etheric forces not only to heal us but also to provide the inner light that will lead us into the realms of the angels.

How can we start to infuse our thinking with light?

There are many steps we can take to achieve this. Let's look at some of them. Perhaps we can explore some exercises that are beneficial. Right now, start thinking over the day you just experienced—in backward order. Can you do this? If you can, wonderful! Now see the whole day in one image like a painting. As you view your day this way, what will jump out at you are any imbalances or incompletions in your life. Do it objectively, as if you were looking at someone else's life. You will see the patterns of your thoughts as never before.

This is an ancient technique that works because it detaches your brain from the usual sequence patterns. In terms of your guardian angel, it enhances the relationship by stimulating you to reflect on areas of your life that might need improvement.

By doing this regularly, you will find that it becomes easier to identify those moments when your thinking has become an obstacle to receiving the help of the angels. You may discover how often you are distracted because of unclear thinking habits. You may realize that you have been operating out of unhealthy emotional states. Eventually you will observe that the nature of your thoughts determines all the interactions in your life. Even though the angel will be able to encourage you in making choices, what actually comes from the outer world to you is the result of your specific thinking habits.

As we prepare ourselves for the next century, we need to be aware that specific factors are becoming part of the decision-making process. We will either expand our freedom in such a way that we can cooperate with heavenly thought, or we will lose our identities by becoming automatic response mechanisms for the rebellious forces opposing God. However, we can work to avert this loss of identity by expanding the process of decision making.

Let us take the exercise I suggested a step further. Instead of only observing our thoughts in the past, it is possible for us to see the effects of our thoughts in the future. Look at your complete life as you would a movie. This time fast-forward to the future, and then play it backward. You will be able to see the results of your thoughts in your life and the surrounding world.

Let's try it. Think ahead years from this moment. Picture yourself in bed about to go to sleep at the end of the day. Now think back over your day. Be creative and don't judge what you envision. Then think back over as much of the year as you can. Images will take shape in your mind. You will be able to sense if you are in harmony with the direction toward which your angels are guiding you.

What is actually occurring here? You are operating with a spiritual part of your brain that you normally do not use. This type of thinking will help in the development of discernment as well as creating a new type of inner freedom from thoughts and ideas impressed on us by the society in which we live.

Here is another helper in making decisions: *do not sit around and ask your angel what to do.* The guardian angel cannot instruct you in this way because it would deprive you of your free will choice. The angel must not directly influence your decisions (with a few exceptions that involve preservation of life). Choices must be made from the level of spiritual consciousness of the individual. This is why so many times we flounder and make poor choices while the angel stands by waiting patiently. What the guardian angel can do, however, is give you a positive sign following your decision. A feeling of exhilaration after making a decision is due to your angel "applauding" your choice. When the choice has been a poor one in terms of spiritual growth, a silence can be felt. It is through this reticence that the angel will encourage its human charge to rethink his or her decision.

If we ask, the guardian angel can do something special to help us make those decisions. The guardian can reveal the consequences of specific choices. If we have developed the ability to think freely and objectively, the angel can transmit inner pictures or a form of knowing that will show the results of the selection before it is made. This is possible because the angel is protector of your personal destiny and will become active, when asked, in ways that will assist you in fulfilling those destined events in your life.

With both these two new ways of perception, one involving expansive thinking in relationship to time and the other through cooperation with the guardian, we can begin to remove major obstacles for the angels.

Our thought processes involve not only the brain but also the whole nervous system. For this reason, most of our thinking is connected to sense perceptions or objects, with the exception of such areas as mathematics or music composition. Missing from our thinking is the ability to go beyond sense perception and develop thought processes that are independent of the sense world. With this type of thinking, we will develop forces that enable us to maneuver in a balanced way through spiritual realms in our sleep as well as in our daytime consciousness.

One of the important results of thinking above sense perception is the experience of having thoughts that are unattached to prior experience or past knowledge. At such moments, one opens the door of consciousness to receive the purest impulses which can stimulate original thinking. This is the pathway for humanity to share creatively with the realms of heaven.

Let us look at an example of how one can become free while developing a new way to think that surpasses sense perception. Suppose we come across a person who has continual difficulties with finances and cannot seem to acquire wealth to the standards of the outer world. Society would view such a person as having failed. Is this really the situation? If we were to spiritualize our thinking, we might develop such thoughts as these from a heavenly perspective:

- Maybe the soul chose to live without our definition of material success in order to achieve inner balance through an alternative experience.

- Maybe the soul chose this path in order to meet with other persons who had similar difficulties and ease their way.

- Maybe the soul was experiencing this hardship to develop compassion necessary for the future.

- Maybe the soul was learning that true success is a spiritual occurrence rather than a material one.

These are merely possibilities to show that oftentimes our thinking does not go far enough. We either make a judgment about the person's life without all the facts or we avoid in-depth thinking. This prevents us from seeing the spiritual truth behind every situation. If we cannot train ourselves to see the spiritual, we will forever be bound to the physical realm and its many illusions.

We need to remember that there is a real connection between our thoughts, sleep, and health. Positive thinking actually will improve sleep and will enhance experiences within the angelic realms. The amount of spiritual thought that one has during the daytime determines access to spiritual realms at night. If you are filled with thoughts of only the material or with negative thinking, it is *impossible* to enter far into the realms of heaven during sleep.

Your thinking will not have created enough light to radiate from your soul during the sleep process. It is important to have this soul light in order to be in the presence of angelic beings. Darkness cannot exist in the realms of heaven, and the darker one's thoughts are, the more limited is the experience of light during sleep.

Conversely, the more you can fill daytime thinking processes with positive images of heaven, and goodness, and other spiritual ideals, the more the angelic ones will welcome your soul during sleep. This means being permitted into the presence of angelic beings that exist on a higher level than your own guardian angel. Such an experience is very nurturing and will stimulate your life the following day.

This is the reason it is so important to spend time releasing thoughts from negativity before entering sleep. Watching a violent television program before sleep, reading a decadent book, or dimming consciousness through alcohol or drugs is the worst thing to do. One of the best things is to pray, review the day, and try to understand what you accomplished from a moral perspective. Wash away all negative thoughts before you enter sleep. If we can individually work to spiritualize our thinking to the point where our access to the heavens is greater during sleep, there is a larger potential to avert these problems.

Why is sleep so important in changing our thinking? I can answer this by explaining the mechanism of sleep in terms of our relationship to the guardian angel and other angelic beings.

Have you ever seen those toys that have a series of balls in successively smaller sizes? Each time you open up a ball there is another inside. The spiritual realms in which we dwell are very similar to this little toy. We have a dense earth surrounded by many other spheres of consciousness, each one within another. On one level they are all together yet separate.

When we go to sleep we expand from our physical body into our spiritual body, moving to the next higher sphere. Our angel is responsible for our safe expansion into these spheres. We can picture the process as if starting from the center of the ball and putting the first layer or covering around it. If your thoughts during the day are filled with light and are of a positive nature, the angel can lead you to the next higher realm, represented by this first enclosure around the ball. The more light that fills your thinking, the more spheres you put around your ball—symbolizing the various angelic realms that surround and envelop you.

Should your thinking be filled with negativity and distrust or denial of God or focused on self with attachment to materialism, the darkness created will bar you from the realms of heaven. This means that you will actually enter by the law of attraction into negative spheres during sleep. Such occasions are difficult for the angel because it cannot accompany you there, *only observe*. Your free will would have accepted the thoughts that pulled you to those dark spheres during sleep. The guardian angel is filled with light and would experience a form of suffocation if it entered these realms with you. The exception is when you find yourself in such darkness and ask for the help of your angel to bring in light. However, a change in thought pattern is required.

A person may remember these experiences or perhaps may have no recollection. However, the effects of negative sleep will still be felt in the attitude and thoughts upon awakening. You could view each day as creating an opportunity for sleep experiences that are healing and inspiring to the soul, or sleep experiences that continuously entrap and erode the soul.

It is also possible that our experiences in the spiritual realm during sleep will be remembered in images which combine to become a dream. These picture memories are different from those dreams that relate to biological processes or allow for the clearing of the unconscious mind. When one has entered into light-filled spiritual realms during sleep and has brought back a memory in the form of images, there is a feeling of wonder about the recollection. The next day there is an impulse to focus on spiritual matters or to rethink an experience or problem from a better perspective.

This leads me to explain another obstacle to the angels in terms of our thinking. We will experience angels according to the image we hold of them. If we envision the guardian angel with very human characteristics, it will appear in that image. If we can perceive the actuality of its body as made up of light, then we will see it in its essence. This explains why there are so many ways in which angels are portrayed.

The problem arises when we hold on to a material interpretation of a spiritual being. This limits the ways in which your angel can appear to you. For example, if you believe that your guardian angel looks one specific way and you are unaware that it is made up of light which takes different forms as necessary, your ability to recognize the activity of your angel is curtailed.

Another area where thoughts can obstruct our experience with angels has to do with confusing the comfort and familiarity of angelic energies with actually being an angel. There are many humans who have developed to the point where their behavior and outlook are at such a beneficent level that they have taken on the manner of an angel. However, they are still human, with a higher level of consciousness than is ordinary. There is a danger in assuming that because of familiarity with angelic energies, one is not a human but an angelic being. First, the assumption interferes with destiny through a denial of one's own path. Second, it leads to a very false experience which tends to pull one away from day-to-day life and cause one to withdraw into self in an unbalanced way. Third, there is denial of the guardian angel, since only humans have guardian angels.

Sadly, Hollywood frequently confuses the difference between highly evolved humans who perform good deeds and actual members of the spiritual hierarchies. Such confusion does not serve the path of wisdom and only encourages a less than serious approach to issues of grave concern to heaven. In very subtle ways lack of spiritual knowledge can affect our thoughts. Perhaps those in the entertainment industry are not intentionally negative but become confused due to lack of information.

It is not difficult for our thoughts to drift away from the positive. However, there usually is a balancing influence within us that will correct the thoughts eventually. When this realignment happens by our own initiative, the guardian angel becomes very active. However, when we tightly hold on to certain negative thoughts, our life situation is not only difficult, but it interferes in the relationship with our guardian angel. Let's look at some of these situations.

One of the thought patterns that permeate our society and that we seem to accept as normal is to blame others. This leads to fighting within families and wars among nations. It denies our own personal responsibility and prevents the angels from improving the situation. *Each time we blame others, a toxic condition is created.* Our society is filled to the brim with the impulse to blame others and penalize them for what is actually our own connection to destiny. This frenzy of blame is indicated by our overflowing courts. Such blaming basically denies that the angel has any heavenly wisdom. Behind any painful experience there is the help and advice of even higher angelic beings who, based upon areas of spiritual growth selected by the soul, assisted the guardian angel in designing the life plan of the human in their care. These angelic ones from the higher hierarchies have tremendous wisdom and compassion in their role as advisors.

We also interfere with the help of angels to heal us when we create a force field of negative thoughts around our body. I once knew a woman who had poisoned herself with negative thoughts to such a point that she was unable to move. She had a coldness in her thinking that jutted out feelings of bitterness. This led to selfish thoughts that encouraged her to reject anything that would be healthy. As a result, her body could not absorb food properly. She became filled with the acids of negative thoughts to the point where she was slowly killing herself. There was an awful smell of fear permeating the house. All this was the direct result of negative thoughts about such important concerns as her deceased husband and the poor relationships she had with other people.

As I began to visit her, it became clear that her guardian angel was having a very difficult time. I started to talk to her about angels, but she was not receptive. She was filled with bitterness. She thought that if angels existed, she should not have all the pain and suffering in her life. This attitude is easy to develop if we are not experiencing the nurturing energy of the angels. It is not possible to experience this energy while our thoughts are negative. When filled with resentful thoughts, we are like porcupines to the angels, making it very difficult for them to come close. It is up to our free will to soften the effects of our thinking.

The solution for this lady was to change the focus of her life from self to others, even in the midst of emotional pain and bodily distress. This enabled her angel to interact on a higher level. Over a period of months, she began to alter the patterns of negative thought and began to smile outwardly in support of her positive attitude. She started believing that angels were real, and as her belief increased, she was able to leave her armchair to use a walker and finally move about with only a cane. She was able to leave her house for the first time in years. This transformation also drew people into her home and opened up new relationships with family members. She was truly experiencing the blessings of heaven as a result of the change in her thinking. Much to the surprise of her doctors, she began to process her food in a healthy way. When death finally came to her, she was an entirely different person filled with radiance and love, ready to enter the spheres of heaven.

The process of removing negative obstacles in their thinking habits takes some people longer than others, but in the end the results are the same: a predominance of hope and joy in the outlook, no matter what the situation, will lead to transformation.

The next step in transforming our thinking is to examine how widespread the limitations are that we place on free thinking. Our global society is filled with "sleepwalkers" who are physically awake but merely going through the motions of life. It has become so easy to accept the forms of thinking of the larger group mind.

We assimilate, both consciously and unconsciously, a tremendous amount of negative thought energy from our culture. It is up to us individually to refuse these influences. If we begin to filter them out, we will have a much easier transition into the new century.

These powerful influences can act as obstacles for our angels. For example, most of us in the United States automatically accept the tradition of working from 9 A.M. to 5 P.M., five days a week, as if it were carved in stone. Until recent years anyone deviating from the pattern was considered strange in our society. The exception, of course, was work done in shifts, such as in factories and hospitals. Today there are people who have refused the template for traditional work, have altered their hours and even the days they work. Some people prefer to work continuously for weeks and then take a longer break; others have begun to share their jobs with another.

The group mind accepts something as the only way and often we all go along with it needlessly. And when we defy the group mind, we experience some of the freedom available to us from the angels. What prevents initiative that will break the mold? Isn't is possible that this is the handiwork of the rebellious angels seeking to dim our will to the point where we become automatons?

We need to evaluate our lives and realize how much of the gobbledygook of the underworld we salute as real. Do you still believe that you have to retire at a specific age? Retire from what? Cease a specific form of work, yes, if it is your choice. But how can we prepare for the most important years of our lives, the latter years, by thinking that we are going to shut down our engines? This false concept was developed basically for economic reasons and to shift the worker base. What have we done by limiting those persons who have the most to offer our society?

The Eastern cultures know the secret. Elder members of society have much wisdom that should be shared. The truth, from an angelic viewpoint, is that as one approaches the years beyond seventy, the veils of heaven are particularly open to the soul. This means that the individual has the opportunity to be of special service to humanity and should begin his or her most important work, which is *to contribute wisdom and experience to the young.*

The process of giving is essential for the elders, or they will wither into hardened crystals of bone and skin filled with sclerotic conditions and unable to move. The flexible and fluid condition of the young is possible in elders provided they are active in giving to others. Just as essential, they should act as prayer monitors for society at large. When the day comes when society gathers our elders together in recognition of their having a special gift that includes access to the heavens to resolve problems with the help of the angels, we will be heading for a civilization based on spiritual truth. It is up to us, as individuals, to fight the group mind that has created some of the images we accept as necessary, such as the abuse and near banishment of the elders instead of creating a place for them in our society.

Every time we free ourselves from such group influence, and the elders rethink the aging process, the negative interference that pulls us too much into the earth is actually transformed. Each time a person realizes that death is a birth into the spiritual world and that preparations should be made by focusing on the spiritual world, *forces of resistance are overcome not only for the individual but for our whole civilization.* Once again, the solution to the activity of the rebellious forces is to look heavenward.

We need to start confronting the vast amount of group-mind images that fill our world. I want to encourage you to compile a list and then compare it with another list of spiritual truths by which you know you can live. These truths will form the principles by which you will operate while dwelling in the midst of thousands of illusions that seek daily to control your free will.

What should you do when you have realized that some part of your life is under the influence of a false group thought form? I suggest that you inwardly reaffirm the opposing truth whenever possible, if only to yourself. For example, we have gradually accepted as real that outer beauty indicates inner health, and thus our emphasis is on developing the most beautiful body before developing the soul. The result is that young children are voluntarily starving themselves in one part of the world, while elsewhere others are dying due to influences they cannot control, either weather, politics, transportation, or war.

We are also giving the message to the young that they will succeed if they first develop a beautiful body that will bring them whatever they want. This order of priorities is in complete contrast to healthy soul development. Going a step further, we have begun to venerate persons with beautiful bodies while ignoring the condition of their souls. Examine the manner in which celebrities and sports figures are treated as gods with exceptional power that impels people to do anything to get close to them, even to touch their garments. Are we not being seduced by the negative polarity that wants us to focus on false bliss?

This certainly does not mean that all persons who enjoy celebrity status due to physical strength or beauty have not developed their souls to reflect the light of God. If they have done so, the veneration projected on them by society should have no meaning and provide no temptation. With such rejection, the rebellious forces are not successful and true beauty can radiate to the world as a gift from heaven.

We are asleep in respect to another area that needs attention. Did you ever notice that when a celebrity is reported to have made some ridiculous or unsound statement in the media, no one challenges what they have said even though it will have a powerful effect on the young? Yet, if the work of a scientist, researcher, or philosopher is discussed, opposite views are reported as a necessity. Why is it that the media report positive contributions to society in such a limited way? This is the kind of question you can begin to ask yourself to gradually become free from the dazed condition of the group mind.

It is time for us to become independent of many illusions that affect how we think, feel, and live. A start is to focus on the group mind images. Eventually you will come to the realization that the rebellious forces have the greatest publicity campaign in the world and we are duped by it over and over. The only solution is to remember that there is one truth that should permeate all you do and all you think: *the love of God is supreme*. If you maintain this focus, the influences from opposition forces will be revealed for the holograms which our society has chosen to call real. When this happens, opposition to your relationship with God becomes transformed into a force of wisdom that will serve the good.

The attention of your life then aligns with that of your guardian angel, which is the development of *love*. When this starts to occur, no longer are the concerns for self overriding the needs of others. Little miracles begin to happen and creative impulses enter life as never before. The exhilaration of joining focus with your angel is beyond description because the angel brings that love force of God directly into your life, having awaited the moment when you were ready to receive it. Those persons who honestly recognize spiritual opposition in their lives start to see things from the angel's viewpoint. This frees the good emissary from heaven to accomplish all sorts of wonderful things.

FEELINGS

Once we have examined the effects of thoughts in creating obstacles in our relationship to the angels, the next step is to understand the role of our feelings. To begin, we need first to examine the origins of our feeling nature from a cosmic viewpoint.

Remember in the creation story when I mentioned the Ancient Moon Period during which the animal kingdom was first created? This was also the time when the astral realm of energy developed. The astral realm is the spiritual energy field that enables us to have feelings. This force has two polarities that can accommodate our feelings—acceptance or rejection, sympathy or antipathy.

The force is woven in and around the physical body, creating a field of colors that can have clarity or density depending on the consciousness of the individual. When we go to sleep at night, it is this field of energy with which we move about in different dimensions with help from the angel. The astral "body" or sheath can be either a vehicle for conscious work with the spiritual world or a dense obstacle due to negative emotions.

One of the reasons many religions and spiritual traditions developed the practice of equanimity is the importance of learning to control emotions while not denying them. The purpose is to gain a balance that will permit the angels to work more closely with you. If, for example, you are filled with feelings of doubt and distrust, it becomes extremely difficult for the angel to communicate in ways you would understand and which would not violate your free will. An image comes to mind of an angel trying to reach the person, similar to an airplane trying to land in the midst of a terrible hurricane. Touchdown is much easier for the angels when we have calm winds and clear skies as far as our emotions are concerned.

We all know too well the destructive effects of negative emotions, but somehow we seem blinded to how we are influenced through our desiring (astral) nature. We can be *seduced by emotions that pull us away from the Divine*, or we can develop positive emotions that will eventually lead to that wonderful state of equanimity.

As I explained in chapter three, there are delinquent angelic beings that have a different goal in mind than that which God has for the development of our lives with free will. These rebellious influences were removed from the heavenly spheres by the Archangel Michael and allowed to interfere with human development on earth *until we reject the negative applications of their influence on our lives and the lives of other beings*.

These beings present obstacles in our feeling life by inflaming our fears, prejudices, distrust, and the sense of insecurity that leads to greed. If we look closely at the animal kingdom, we will see that many of the qualities of the animal reflect emotional states which we may still be dealing with in our lives. For example, we all have the potential to rage like a bull, to be wily as a fox, or slithery as a snake. It is up to us to transform these qualities within our own souls.

The guardian angel does not require perfection in your feelings to be able to help you or work with you. The need is to have the airfield cleared, the way made easier, by your having on a consistent basis more positive emotions than negative emotions. If you have difficulties in working through specific feelings, you can ask the angel to help clear the way. Because of the nature of free will, the angel cannot remove the fog of negativity unless you ask for God's help.

Here are a few symptoms of the presence of obstacles to your relationship with the angels in the area of feeling. These obstacles are the result of succumbing consciously or unconsciously to the rebellious forces of the universe:

- use of feelings to get what one desires

- holding on to past experiences that are negative or fearing the future

- bouncing between extremes of what is liked and disliked

- profanity as an expression of a negative feeling, swearing

- excessive attachment to having or acquiring money

- sex for self—to feel good, more than to share

- fear of change on any level

- excessive attachment to a person or group

- feelings of bitterness or resentment

- lack of compassion for those who suffer

- apathy that prevents being charitable

- fear of not having enough, which leads to manipulation and greed

If you identify these types of feelings or other feelings as present in your life, you will start the process of improving your relationship with the angels of God. Each day complete a checklist for your feelings, as you should for your thoughts. You will find that once you have identified the primary negative feelings that are affecting your life, you can begin to replace them with more positive feelings.

While working with angels, I find that it is especially good to follow this practice daily, often prior to sleep. Sometimes it is more effective in the morning, depending upon events. It is like a pilot doing a check on the instrument panel prior to takeoff. I know if I am feeling upset about something or depressed even by weather conditions, it affects my ability to work. Sometimes the choice is to select the kind of tasks I can do that will help lift the feeling, and it usually works. Over and over, I have seen that just by making a conscious effort to transform my feelings, I can clear the way for the angels to participate more fully in everything I do.

Another method I have for identifying any emotional obstacle between myself and the higher worlds is to make a list of recent events in my life that may be the source of irritation or negative feeling. Oftentimes, we blame one event or person and the cause is something entirely different.

Additional help may be needed to balance this feeling nature, sometimes in the form of prescribed medication. This type of help may be a necessity for certain individuals. However, persons who have a belief in God and the desire to transform their life can also ask their angel to help balance out the emotions. I have seen amazing changes in the inner life of people who have begun to work with their angel. As the angel responds and the individual's energies become clearer, life itself improves because the angel is no longer restricted.

ACTIONS

Sometimes it is easier for someone to realize that thoughts or feelings can interfere with our relationship to the angels than it is to examine the blocking effects of actions and inappropriate use of will. This is because we rarely spend time analyzing the nature of our deeds or becoming aware of the effects of our will. It is understandable because our will activity that stimulates actions is basically unconscious. Since it is unconscious, it is one of the more difficult areas to identify.

If you wish to discover the obstacles to the angels created by your deeds, examine whether you have any of these symptoms:

- jobs that are not connected to who you really are or what is best for your spiritual growth

- meaningless actions

- laziness and inactivity

- expressions of violence, including how we drive

- lack of courtesy and genuine respect among family members and work associates

- acceptance of insincere acts as being necessary in life, such as certain gift-giving and generalized greetings

- lack of acts arising out of initiative and higher ideals

- endorsing violence by attending or participating in recreational activities that involve violence

- being unaware of the realm of nature when moving about from place to place or while resting

- signing contractual agreements based on greed or insecurity, whether a marriage or a business contract

- initiating any action that is a violation of one's own spiritual principles

Sometimes our angel will try and show us the problem in different ways including dreams. It is important that we heed such inner cautions. I have a story to illustrate the intricate connections between our actions or lack of action and the inner world.

I knew a woman who had a cute small dog. She would go about with this little black dog and let the dog create a chaotic atmosphere wherever it went. People noticed that the owner, who was very spiritually minded but considered to be weak in the area of decisive action, never seemed to confront the dog. It was as if they were equals, and the owner did not dare to act as master and require proper behavior. The situation became worse for the owner, and more people noticed that there seemed to be a connection between the nervous tension of the animal and that of the owner, yet no action was being taken to improve the situation.

Along with this outer condition, there was inner confusion in the owner's mind about what work to do. She had made a decision to work in a particular creative stream, and it was clear that she had both talent and knowledge. However, she avoided taking the action of working on the project. Part of this was fear that it was too much work, especially since she had recently retired from the job she had held for thirty years.

The woman had a dream that she was holding a snake with a banana peel. She realized that the peel would not hold the head of the snake, and it bit her.

The morning after the dream she came to visit me for the day. Shortly after her arrival, another visitor arrived earlier than expected, and we went out on the deck to make some necessary decisions while the lady with the dog put her animal in her car to minimize chaos.

Suddenly, the dog was dashing about the lawn, with the lady running behind. The dog had jumped out of the car window and would not come to the owner. Instead, it ran around and dashed in a disruptive way across the deck where my other guest and I were talking. Suddenly I heard a vicious snarling and a yell. The little dog had been caught by the owner and had bitten her badly on the hand. There were open puncture marks, and blood; the dog had held on with its teeth.

I realized that there was a serious rift in the relationship between the dog and its owner. My friend went inside with my other guest to cleanse and bandage the injury. She was quite shaken and very upset with the dog. Meanwhile, it was clear that the inner and outer worlds of the owner were merging. The refusal to discipline the animal, to take necessary action in a timely way, had led to the release of negative energy. During that same week, my friend had experienced a feeling of depression resulting from not taking necessary action relating to a spiritual commitment.

Having some experience working with animals, I took the little black dog aside and began to discipline it immediately. I knew that the biting had been almost reflexive. The problem was that the little dog had no respect for humans. Instead, the dog viewed humans as agents who would give it whatever it wanted. The owner had developed this condition in the dog by not teaching it to obey.

The little dog began to behave as I worked with it. When I came inside to check on the condition of the owner, she mentioned that she had dreamt of being bitten the night before. We talked about the dream, and she seemed to realize that there was a serious connection between the negative experience of the attack and her lack of action appropriate to the situation's demand. The hand would heal, and the owner would now start serious training with the animal. Along with that, she would begin training herself by setting goals and parameters for her work.

I have selected this incident to show how *the angels try to help us avert pain, if we will only heed their cautions and take necessary action.* The owner of the little dog had been conscious of the difficult behavior of the animal for the past year and had let things slide. She had also been aware of her problem with making decisions and following through with them. Here, also, little action had been taken to remedy this inner condition. If we do not act in a timely manner to transform the obstacles to our spiritual life but instead let things slide and continue avoidance policies, we will eventually be confronted with a "bite from the serpent." This symbolically represents the influence of negative spiritual forces or rebellious angels—operating in this case in the will area of the owner and creating unbalanced behavior by an innocent animal. It is always up to us humans to bring out the highest positive responses in any pets we have in our care.

One very prevalent obstacle that many of us experience is the effect of distractions on our ability to accomplish something we set out to do. Frequently we may have positive thoughts, feelings, and will impulses. Yet, as we begin to translate these areas into action, universal forces of opposition interfere. This is especially true when one seeks to accomplish deeds based solely on the will of God. Often the interference is subtle but very powerful. The image that comes to mind is of a person trying to thread a needle. Just at the moment when the thread is about to enter the hole the person's arm is bumped and she has to start all over.

The example of this interference or distraction is familiar to many artists and writers. I remember many years ago when I was painting in my studio, I would turn off all the phones and put up a "do not disturb" sign on the front door. One day while I was painting, an angel revealed to me that I did not need to close myself off from the world. Only those persons who wanted to reach me would telephone; so I reconnected the phones and took down the sign. For many years now, I find that only real spiritual emergencies that do need my attention interrupt my painting time, and I am able to go back to the piece easily.

However, I find it is different when writing. I think this is because of the use of words, the technology of computers and even typewriters. Distractions have occurred in the writing of this book that are the most absurd, despite my pleading for the heavens to protect the process. I realized that there was a reason for this experience, and it became clear I needed to encounter this firsthand so that I could write about it more clearly.

The situation of repeated distractions is the symptom of our time. What used to be news stories flashed in one minute are now down to five-second flashes. The media business is convinced that our attention span is now down to seconds and, to be sure to get our attention, bombards us with messages at increasing speeds before we can even comprehend, let alone digest, the one that just flashed by. Truly, we are living in vehicles of consciousness that are traveling at a hundred miles an hour. It is no wonder that relationships are suffering. Basically, there is no time to focus on the development of human interaction much less utilize the time needed to focus on the angels.

I am reminded of past interviews with certain news reporters. As the popularity of angels expanded, more requests would come for me to do an interview. Over and over, I realized that the reporter was basically assigned the task by an editor, and both of them truly knew almost nothing about the subject of angels. I was being utilized to provide them with a crash course on angels. They also wanted me to condense the workings of the universe into one or two sentences. Often after such an interview, I felt that I had been violated for the sale of the written word. These days I am wiser and have placed some safeguards on my work to avoid as much distortion in its message as possible.

With those reporters who did some real research other than reading other news articles, I had an opportunity to explain the significance of the current interest in angels. Those writers created responsible articles that are a tribute to the heavens. Each one of their articles is lengthy and unable to be broken down into sound bites which prevent a complete and accurate meaning.

To go back to the subject of the distractions we face in being creative, this is oftentimes a strengthening experience because it firms up the determination to complete a project. However, it can also weaken the resolve and courage to do the work. I found that sometimes the best way to overcome these distractions was to identify whether they originated from the outer world or from within myself. Those distractions that involved the outer world, such as a door-to-door salesman coming to the house unannounced to offer something I would never purchase, were the most difficult type. The break in attention was jarring. I had to focus on his request and say that I could not speak to him. That act of negation shifted the energies. I recognized that possibly the rebellious forces would have timed the uninvited solicitation to arrive when I was working rather than at another time. It is interesting to note that my house is not easy to locate.

Distractions originating within myself rather than in external sources I identified as the polarity either to become caught in unnecessary details or to start thinking of a long-deserved vacation. I began to have pictures entering my mind of something I have desired for many years yet never experienced: a cruise on a fabulously plush ocean liner. Each time the interruption came, I would have pictures of the balcony I would lean against, the view of the sea, the lack of interruptions, and the different parts of the world I would like to visit. Before long, I found myself thinking about cruising around the world, a distraction that had very little connection to reality. What was I doing? My own dragon was distracting me from the work at hand by tempting me with thoughts of something I did not even know beforehand that I desired. It was unimportant if I ever even went on such a journey. I was being taken on the journey in pictures that would lure me away from my work, even if only for a few seconds. The rebellious angels knew that I would not consciously stop my work for God, but I might accept that particular form of distraction because of years of extremely difficult work schedules.

Psychologists might say that it was healthy to take a break from such intense creative work and that thinking about cruising around the world would be a stress release. I do not agree. I think we are all seduced away from our work continually in small distracting ways and we need to confront them. What I did to stop the interference, to transform the influence into a positive one, was to actually agree to plan a short trip out of town, even if only for a weekend. *By taking responsive action*, I stopped the interference. Should the day come when I actually take a cruise somewhere, I will know that it was the work of the heavens, not of the rebellious ones.

The problem of distractions in writing proved to be quite valuable to me, and by confronting them one by one I became stronger, while at the same time much more discerning about priorities. I recognized that the angels in my own life had allowed me to experience the interference so that I could be more sensitive to delays by others. Also, it provided an experience that I could share with you.

One of the greatest problems that faces us as we seek to transform ourselves and our world so that we can align ourselves with the good angels is how to make healthy decisions. Most of our choices that lead to actions are effected on the basis of emotions or intellectual thought processes. Sometimes, it is just will impulse alone. There is another route to decision-making that is far more effective and that leads to better results. It is what I call a tripod agreement.

I make sure that when making a decision there are three components which have to be in agreement. This constitutes the tripod agreement. The components are:

How do I *feel* about the choices ahead?

What do I *think* about the choices?

What action am I *willing* to take?

If any one of these components—feeling, thinking, and willing—leads to a negative answer, I take it as an indication that the decision needs to be postponed or examined in greater detail. More information may be necessary in order to arrive at a positive response. Also, I realize that if there is no harmony between feeling and thought about an idea, it is likely that any action will be eventually undermined by the subconscious, which houses both positive and negative aspects of will.

If you look back over some of the unsuccessful decisions of your life, you will probably find that you did not have tripod agreement basing your decision.

This may be a good moment to mention to you that there is much confusion about how we should go about making decisions when we have a guardian angel. I know people who will not do anything until they "hear" their angel tell them what to do. I caution against this way of taking action in life because it is open to illusion. Rather, consider this thought: under Divine law your guardian angel cannot interfere with free will, or free choice, which is an inherent part of the spiritual progression of a soul. If the angel told you everything to do, you would become an automaton, and that is not the intention of the hierarchies. Decisions must arise out of your free will.

The good news is that even though your angel will not order you specifically, except with loud warnings that are to protect the safety of the physical body (like "stop" before falling over a cliff), the angel will have prepared you ahead of time through life experiences to be able to make the right decision. The necessary information is there or is available. The important aspect to remember is that it is in the power of the guardian angel to confirm the validity of your decision after it has been made. The angel can also indicate that it was an unwise decision, thus encouraging you to rethink the subject. Many of us have experienced a rush of delight after making a decision; it feels almost like a flight of birds taking off into the air. Likewise, when an error in decision has been made, there is an awful stillness, a dead feeling, that one cannot seem to shake. If the decision is not undone immediately, then resistance can set in and things begin to get more and more muddled. The angel oftentimes is hoping that the decision will be changed before action goes too far.

The value of making decisions on the basis of a tripod agreement is that this act itself disengages you from the negative influences and makes it so much easier for the angel to help avert problems in your life without overcoming your free choice.

I think a wonderful example of this is when we plan trips. Many people have thoughts about taking a special vacation, and even more have desires to do so but do not think about it in depth. The only way to achieve such a trip is to take action, which might be as simple as circling a date on the calendar and contacting a travel agent. If one does not act, then the goal, whether it be a trip or specific service to the Divine, will not occur.

So often, people ask me how I am able to achieve the many things I have done so far in my life. My response is that I definitely seek to listen to advice from the heavens, but I also take action when I have an idea and it feels right. I do not worry about the success of the project, or trip, until it is actually under way. This lesson I learned years ago when I studied the lives of creative people such as Beethoven, whom I especially love. One day it became so clear in the simplest way that he would never have written any beautiful symphonies for the world to hear over the centuries if he had not reached for that first piece of paper. If he had not done so, all that gorgeous music would be carried around in his soul and perhaps taken back into the heavens upon his death.

We need to recognize the power of our deeds and the influence on our lives from lack of action and reflect on how inaction interferes with the guiding work of our angel.

Many achievements in transformation become possible with positive support from the angels. I call this the time when one can learn to "walk on water." If we are in harmony with our angels and radiate the love of God, we can develop an inner mind picture which I describe as being able to metaphorically walk across water. First, start out envisioning your body submerged up to the neck in water. Then raise yourself out of and above the water, letting your angel lift you from your troubles. Begin to see yourself rise and gradually move across the water. This really can happen when you are in harmony with the angels. If you are influenced by negative limitations, liftoff is difficult if not impossible. Try it. You may begin to understand the inner meaning of the Bible story of Jesus Christ's walk upon the water as He approached His disciples in their fishing boat during a storm. Peter started to walk toward Him. But when he looked down and lost his belief in what was happening, he began to sink.

Remember, as soon as you doubt Divine support, you will sink back into the troubled waters of your life. It is very similar to a dream of flying. When you realize that you are indeed in flight but question how it is possible, you no longer fly. Practice walking on the waters of your mind and your faith in the heavens will expand. This faith will lead to a major transformation.

The secret of the perseverance of the saints and the lasting impact of great explorers, composers, artists, scientists, and others is that they knew that they would never be successful if they accepted as truth the voices that said their goal was impossible to achieve. They also learned to love the process toward the goal as much as the goal itself, thus bringing a great deal of love energy, or God force, directly into the work process. When the process, which is connected to time, receives the same amount of love as the goal, which is timeless, the threshold to heaven has opened. The obstacles have ceased to have impact and a new way of relating to the heavens has begun.

SOME SUGGESTIONS

Here is how we can begin to work with the angels of God to counteract interference from the rebellious in our society at large:

- When you see acts of violence reported in the world, or highlighted for entertainment purposes almost to the point of veneration, discern the influence but do not judge the people who do such deeds. Remember that they are being influenced by angelic forces of rebellion, and you also enter this influence if you judge the person rather than the source. At the same time, ask yourself if you are violent in any way in your life, even your thoughts. If you agree to see violence for entertainment, are you not responsible in part for its place in our society?

- Make commitments to the animal kingdom that are sincere and lasting. Is not the pet you have connected directly to God? When you treat pets as disposable or do not live with them in a responsible way, this has a disrupting effect on the heavens. Remember that the animals are closely connected to the angelic realms. It is up to us if we want to be under the influence of the rebellious forces in terms of our relationships with animals.

- When you see exhibitionism of depraved soul conditions such as the current rage on many television shows, refuse to let the images have your attention. Bless the souls involved while at the same time changing your own focus. Realize that such persons are playing out the delinquent parts of our group consciousness. Look with compassion on the people and, again, remember that the problem is the rebellious angelic influences from which the people need to free themselves.

- When you are ill with a virus, recognize that a spiritual imbalance has occurred that can be treated only through an infusion of the force that breaks up the crystalline action of the viruses and that is *love*. If you come down with the flu, don't only drink lots of fluids and get bed rest, but consciously view where your life is out of balance and make decisions to reestablish harmony within yourself and with God.

- If anyone wants to give you instant enlightenment or a way to God consciousness without doing serious inner work, start walking away. The same applies to working with angels. If the major topic is not God when dealing with angels, you might be responding to the advertising of the underworld. Again, there should not be a judgment on the person but a recognition of the source.

- Go to different churches and temples to see firsthand how others experience their religion. Do it with sincerity, and the experience of open acceptance will help the angels bring religious harmony to the world.

- When you feel gripped by the demands of time and rush about life from task to task, stop periodically and get off the carousel of illusions. We don't need to walk down the street so fast and so unconsciously that we bump into other people. We don't have to forfeit our lives for speed on the highways. The carousel of endless duties spins faster and faster until we realize that it is possible to step off, even if all the rest of society chooses to remain.

- Do an inventory of your interests, activities, and responsibilities and see if they are consistent with your spiritual ideals. If not, perhaps it is time to take action and realign your life with the truth of who you really are. If everyone would do this simple check on a regular basis, our civilization would fulfill the wonderful potential that awaits us if we can only correct our priorities.

As you begin to work with some of these social conditions, I encourage you to remember that *the most widespread disease of our times is apathy connected to a severe case of hopelessness.* If we give in to this, the rebellious angels will have succeeded in detouring God's children from the pathway home. If the task of changing our world seems almost impossible, remember to view life from the perspective of heaven. In those realms anything can be achieved through focus as long as it is in harmony with the will of God. Your guardian angel will bring you to a level of hope if you will decide to overcome the opposition forces. *It is time to confront the dragon*—with wisdom, strength, and love.

Chapter Five

SLAYING THE DRAGON

Now that you have identified obstacles in your relationship with the guardian angels, it is time to conquer the major source of spiritual rebellion operating in your inner life. Ancient traditions and theology that mention the overcoming of darkness by courage, love, and light refer to this process as "the slaying of the dragon."

In the new millennium, we can approach the conquest of spiritual rebellion under a new image of transformation. The old picture of Saint George slaying the dragon will give way to a more loving image that has the same power of light over darkness but includes creativity and freedom. It is to "tame the dragon" through love and wisdom to where its activity will change from negative to positive.

The dragon will never truly die, so we cannot slay it. Rather, we can transform the darkness into light through conscious love and wisdom. During this process remember that your guardian angel is ever present and quite willing to help if you ask. You are always protected by an angel as long as you love God. Above all, the angel supports the transformation of the dragon.

THE DRAGON TALE

Everyone has a dragon, each with its own color and size. Some are black, some dark brown, some a deep green, and others have different colors. Your dragon may be very tall or very long, but it is most assuredly strong. All the dragons that are not tamed go about in the neighborhood and visit with other dragons. During their romping and playing, property is destroyed, and sometimes people are stepped on even without the dragon's awareness. These dragons have a wonderful time playing with one another. They go about wherever they want to visit with one another.

If you decide to tame your dragon, you need first to build a corral in your backyard or an area in the woods. Make the corral very tall so that the dragon cannot look over the top. Then you will need to capture the dragon. Go and get a piece of rope made of sunlight and throw it around his neck. It will take a special knot to hold the dragon while you walk him back home or to the woods. The dragon will not want to go into the corral but you must not give in. Be strong, and eventually he will go into the corral.

The rebellious one will hiss and spit fire in anger at being contained. Don't be fearful. Instead, tell the dragon that he is no longer free to roam and play with other dragons. When it is time to feed him, bring him a golden bowl filled with positive thoughts. He will probably kick the bowl or spit out the contents. Just ignore him and go away. Gradually, he will become hungry for his old meal of negative thoughts and will demand that you bring it to him. Offer him another golden bowl of goodness. He may refuse again, but when he realizes that there is no other food coming, he will start to taste it. At first it will be strange to him, but hunger will force him to eat. At the same time, start talking to him. He is becoming lonely because there are no other dragons to play with. Here too he will ignore you at first, but when he realizes you are the only one he can talk to, he will start to listen.

As the days go by, his fire spitting will become less. Visit the corral and start to beautify it. Bring out pearls, rubies, emeralds, and other jewels and embed them in the corral. As he becomes more willing to converse with you, spend more time with him talking over his problems and giving positive responses. You will find that because he is now eating only the food from the golden bowl, he is becoming pleasant to be around. Your conversations increase in friendliness, and he starts to tell you all sorts of wonderful things. He explains why certain things have happened in your life and why certain people are the way they are. One day you realize that you left the gate open but he did not wander out. He likes his new friend and his new life. Your dragon has become transformed into a helping source of wisdom and strength and no longer seeks to bring harm to the world.

This tale teaches the principles of transformation that can only be accomplished through replacement of the negative with the positive on all levels. It also speaks of the need to be courageous and loving even to those resistant parts of ourselves.

I have known people who were totally unaware of their dragon's effect on their own lives and the lives of others. Could it be that many painful and debilitating illnesses such as alcoholism, drug dependence, and other addictions existed in the individual's life even before the substances were ever taken because he or she felt powerless to control his or her dragon? Perhaps the pain that our society tries to dim through its numbing excesses is in reality an attempt to deny the presence of the dragon.

To fully understand the nature of this dragon, you must realize that even though its specific activities differ with each person, there are basically two polarities in which it operates. The first direction causes the human to become egotistical, to think of self above others, and to want to escape from daily life and its demands into false experiences of synthetic bliss, such as drugs. The second direction leads the human to the experience of fear, greed, hatred, and a hardening of his or her whole system. These two polarities can pull on us at the same time—which might cause one to harden a personal experience, such as a religious feeling, into a justification to dismiss or even annihilate other persons who do not maintain the same viewpoint.

It is true that these polarities that tempt humanity are not in reality a force like magnetism. Their activity is the result of many negative spiritual beings who are operating for the fallen angels, those angels who continue to refuse the will of God and, in fact, seek to destroy humanity's relationship with the Creator. If the rebellious ones are successful, they will establish their own kingdoms in which humans will be nothing more than slaves to their desires. Thankfully, as each human being becomes conscious of the activities of these rebellious influences, the process of true freedom begins. This freedom is achieved by rejecting the offerings of the underworld and accepting the offerings of the angels of God.

SOME SPECIFICS

If you have identified some of your own personal hindrances, as a first step, it is then a good idea to analyze whether those obstacles tend more to pull you away from humanity and caring for the earth or to make you excessively bound to the earth to the point where the hardening processes have tightened your life. Evaluate where your focus is most of the time. Are your thinking and your actions connected to the betterment of human life, to helping yourself and others strengthen their connection to God? Or is the focus of your life mainly directed to personal pleasure and gain? Have you perhaps become enslaved in the working world solely to maintain ownership of material possessions? Figure out how much time is spent on inward activity with your guardian angel and how much is devoted to demands of an illusionary nature. Once you do the tally, the resolution of the situation can start.

If you find that the majority of your energies are directed toward an egotistical development of self (this is the time to be really honest), then balance this by giving yourself some grounding experiences. Begin a program of action with people in extreme need, such as the homeless or the dying, that does not involve money. Give your energy which has been focused on your own life to the lives of others. This activity will awaken a sense of compassion that will help your angel establish a balance in your life while at the same time giving you an opportunity to connect with others in such a way that you should feel humbled. If you become proud of the work you do and enjoy praise from those you help, you may as well stop. If will only create additional problems between you and the guardian angel. If you think that writing a check is the proper response, think again. In such an instance, you have only reassigned a task that needs to be done by you personally. Birth, death, and truly helping another directly are the three things that you can never hire another to do in place of doing them yourself.

What if your focus is in the other direction, more toward an attachment to materialism? Are you afraid of losing security, money, or even health? The need here is for your viewpoint to be expanded. Most individuals with this polarity problem do not look upward sufficiently. To achieve this and reverse the hardening process that can eventually make one quite ill, seek out an activity that will lift your thoughts. One of the best ways is to pray for others who are in need and do so in a serious fashion. As one begins to pray consistently for another person to receive help, a change occurs in the heart. You will find that your thinking becomes more positive and even hopeful. The fear and anger that restricted your life begin to diminish. This is because the guardian angel always helps one who sincerely asks God to help another without being judgmental. You can't succeed at this if you are praying for a friend to change his or her ways. That is control. Instead, pray for blessings in the lives of all you know. When you get to be good at it, pray for those who do not know God's love. You might even pray for blessings for your neighbors or those who work to lead our nation.

What this will do is free you from the belief that material existence is the real security in life. You will directly experience how the will of God can supersede anything if one prays in an unselfish manner and is willing to accept that the final decision to effect change or not to effect change originates from the Creator.

I once knew a person who was able to tame her dragon by establishing new rules of focus for herself. She had for many years suffered with a very difficult relationship with her daughter-in-law, but there was a wonderful grandchild that she adored. The problem between the woman and her daughter-in-law had to do with miscommunication and insecurity on both sides. The grandmother realized that if anything was to be done to improve their relationship, she needed to ask for help from the angels. As part of the process, she became aware that she had become too anxious and controlling, basically out of fear of rejection. The grandmother began conscious work to see the good in her daughter-in-law on a much higher level and designed specific activities that would demonstrate her affection in a way that was not controlling. Soon she spoke about how differently she felt about the whole situation. She was actually even willing to release her connection with the grandchild. Above all, she wanted to infuse the relationship with higher energies. The good news is that the affiliation opened a few weeks later, and the two women began a friendship that brought new life to everyone. The grandmother's own life circumstances improved, and important changes took place smoothly, such as the sale of a house and a move to a long-awaited place in the sun. It took her only a matter of days to loosen the grip of the rebellious forces once she began without fear to think of others in a generous, accepting way.

Commitment and Responsibility

The dragon forces that make us fearful and rigid also have a paralyzing effect. Oftentimes these influences don't have to inspire negative action. Rather, they encourage lack of action. This is one of the most prevalent situations, especially with spiritually minded people. Through the years I have met many individuals who have libraries full of spiritual books and pride themselves on being very learned about how to develop a relationship with God. They attend workshop after workshop and come home with notebooks bulging. Sadly, the good intention to contribute to the outer world never goes beyond study of self, and actual deeds do not occur. Eventually such a person feels stuck or unnourished even with the inner spiritual work, and doesn't understand why.

What has really occurred is that the focus of the individual was diverted away from possible deeds that would help civilization and directed toward self-development where personal desire is often quite strong. By deflecting the focus of the individual, the rebellious angels achieve their silent goal of preventing humanity from becoming free and able to consciously work with the angels of God.

I remember a young man who attended some of my classes and participated in social events held by my organization. He was delighted to attend, chat with people, bring flowers, and even assist in preparing food. But I began to notice that he dashed off while others were helping with the cleanup. I dismissed it as insignificant. One day, however, as we began working on a particular project that had potential global significance, he seemed resistant. Finally, I realized that he had never made a commitment to actually work but preferred to go about life as if it were a party in progress. As he did at a party, he would engage in the entertaining aspect, but he found the hard work behind the scenes difficult despite his good intentions. The angels lose potential workers when this situation exists. Positive intentions must be carried into deeds on some level. Sadly, such lack of action results in additional work and responsibility for other people.

Many of us wonder why our prayers are not immediately answered for a specific problem. Oftentimes, they have been answered, but the delivery route, which must come through humans in most cases, has been interrupted by lack of action. We are so aware of the effects of negative actions that I think most of us, individually, try to prevent them. *However, as a society we are unaware of how our lack of correct action serves the rebellious forces.*

So how do we achieve correct action that helps the delivery system of the angels? A start might be to make real commitments that have meaning. Most individuals in our society break their word many times a day. The code of honor is gone. In this age of technological wonder where we have an excess of written contracts, we have lost the meaning behind the word. When a person gives his or her word about something, it is supposed to be that person's truth in verbal form for an intended act. When this word is violated, language, which is of great importance to the angels of

God, has been taken under the influence of the rebellious forces. Each time that we fail to keep our word, whether spoken or written, we have caused interference in the heavens. One's word is meant to be sacred, to be honored. When it is not, the spiritual origins of the words spoken are defiled.

One of the reasons that our society has become so filled with broken words and broken agreements is that the rebellious forces are the great masters at this negative skill. The angels of darkness promise humanity all sorts of things in order to gain control. They will go to any end to deceive or to justify or to twist the original intent of an agreement. If we wish to transform this dragon that affects us all, we need to begin to value our words. This means not only speaking the truth but also removing excess words from our expressions with one another. Greetings that are insincere or automatic interfere with the angels of light. In a conscious way, find something truthful to say to a person you greet.

Listen to others as if you were hearing the voice of God speaking out of their mouths. This puts real value back into the communication process, reveals the nonessentials quickly, and enables one to understand other people in a remarkably clear way. Most of us do not listen, but are busy preparing our response to a particular word we heard the other person say. We need to hear the complete thought. If you begin to really listen to others, you develop a sense of respect for the words used to communicate.

Many of our distortions in society arise from the poor use of words that no longer have any connection with the heavens. If we are statistically so high in multiple divorce rates for individuals who have given very serious verbal and written commitments to one another, it is a natural consequence of having lost the meaning of our words. The further and further away our actions are from the words we speak and the commitments we have made, the more fog we create between ourselves and the angelic realms.

Another aspect of commitment should be mentioned. That is the widespread fear that people have in making real commitments to change or to taking beneficial actions. This is often due to an inner laziness and a preference for having others take initiative. Yes, there are exceptions. There are also many initiatives that start out with good intentions. However, when hard work is involved, the priorities change. On a spiritual level, this is one of the most serious problems we face. Lethargy has led to the demise of many civilizations before this time.

If the adversary forces want to destroy something, there are two ways they can be successful. They can pull on the soul to convince the person not to take action or they can encourage an inappropriate act. When opposing those forces, it is easier to correct actions that are in error than it is to unfreeze a condition of soul paralysis. Be sure to accept responsibility for your life and for our planet. Don't expect other people to be the ones to take action.

Oftentimes people who want to take action to help the world ask me how they can find out what their angel wants them to do. If that is the approach they take to their guardian angel, they will never get an answer. *Angels can only endorse or remain silent after we make our commitments.* If your angel were to direct you to make a specific commitment, you would not be using your free will. Sometimes the rebellious ones create confusion so that a person is actually afraid to make a choice or a commitment and then follow it. You can see how pervasive the problem is of humanity being detoured into sins of omission. This interference can be transformed by refusing to agree to anything that we truly cannot accept in our thoughts or our feelings, or that we are unwilling to put into action.

The transformation of your inner dragon is not an easy process. As soon as progress seems to have been made, there are new opportunities to confront your old darkness. Take along a package of humor as you work in this area. You will find that humor has an amazing effect on the dragons we encounter—whether our own or those from another source. I think this is because true humor is connected to fluidic release of kindness. Such an energy has a disconcerting effect on the dragon.

Chapter Six

THE ANGELS' CUP

The angels do not have checkbooks! This situation means that guardian angels work through people to bring the abundance which God intends for humanity. Unfortunately, the area of money is seriously in danger of total control by the rebellious angels. The spiritual emissaries of God are in real need of an awakened humanity that can transform this critical part of our lives.

In fact, good impulses that help our world have been sabotaged by the influence of rebellious angels. They do this by cutting off money resources at an essential time or subverting projects into ideals different from those which will help bring about alignment with God.

A week does not go by without my hearing one person or another mention they wished they had enough money to help others the way they would like to. For persons who have sincere charitable goals in mind, this is especially frustrating. Other people mention that they lack time or energy for specific tasks that will help to improve civilization.

Monetary shortages are not the will of God. The source of this problem is a lack of spiritual energy. The angels will provide us with more than we will ever need if we can just learn about the process and what to do to receive this energy. As a start, let's redefine money.

Mistakenly, people separate money from their spiritual life. I know so many instances in which spiritually conscious people will talk about almost anything in the universe, but not money. Yes, there are some who are obsessed with the subject, but that is also an imbalance. The problem is never money itself but the *attachment* to having, acquiring, or not-having money. It often surprises people to hear that persons who focus continuously on how little they have are experiencing the same attachment to money as those who hoard it excessively for personal use. When you hear two such persons talking together, you know that both are followers of money as their god rather than the real Creator.

The attachment is the problem that needs to be addressed. We can release ourselves by developing a new perspective. To achieve this, I suggest a simple exercise: substitute the word "energy" for money every time you have a transaction. For example, when you are concerned that there might not be enough money in the bank to pay a bill, say to yourself that you are short on spiritual energy. Things will look quite different. The incentive will come to focus on the true source of all abundance, your relationship to God.

What if one who deals in millions and is fascinated by the illusionary power of money begins to think in a way that will free him or her from control by rebellious angels? Such persons might say to themselves that they are holding on to a tremendous amount of energy and there was conscious effort to acquire even more. The question should come to mind: is the energy truly being distributed or released in harmony with spiritual law, or is it being contained to the point where it will implode upon itself?

And what about debt? We could also look at this as a repayment of energies. When we have excessive personal debt, this is an indicator that it is time to give out more personal energy to the world around in addition to fulfilling the actual financial commitment. Sure enough, people who are overloaded with debts almost always say how they have barely enough for themselves, so how can they give to anyone else? Yet, the world is full of books that document cases in which people who began to help others started to have a change in their financial status.

If we bring this thinking to the level of our national debt, it becomes very interesting. Our government has gradually run out of energy and has had to borrow to operate. What does this mean spiritually? Could it be that the energy that started our country— the principles and good intentions—has been siphoned off by the rebellious forces? If this is the case, would not the solution be for our government to reevaluate its priorities so that the energy system, the money system, can be realigned?

It is true that at each election we seek to reestablish certain priorities in the political process. Somehow our legal actions and our decisions related to "rights" have come under the influence of money in many areas of our society. Our energy system has become compromised. To realign the system, *both* our government and individuals need to free up energy in other areas, similar to the way a person who lives hand to mouth can start doing something for others around them. I do not mean that our nation should hand out more money. Rather, we are lacking in deposits of energy to our spiritual bank account. These deposits, which affect the monetary situation of our country, can be made by individuals contributing time and care to their communities, and doing the same on a national level and international level. We Americans should contribute to the spiritual account by sharing with our people and others *the principle of freedom under which we were established as a nation*. Religious choice and tolerance of the varieties of paths to God are also an offering that our nation and its people can give.

If you spend even a few moments thinking about these possibilities, you will contribute to the group consciousness of our nation. Whatever energy level you have, there is some contribution you can make.

I think we are very good as a people when it comes to disaster relief. That is something we understand because it involves specific needs for food, shelter, blood, medicine, and even labor. The response is healthy and sincere. Now, however, we need to respond to the monetary (energy) crisis that is already upon us. There is no way to heal the situation by furthering the process that drains the energy. To stop the siphoning off of our national energy, individuals must become more responsible for the energy they use in their own lives, the areas in which major focus is placed. If 95 percent of the time one is working to acquire material possessions or pay for activities of pleasure, there is a severe imbalance that has contributed to national monetary problems.

We need to understand that the angels consider money an illusion until humanity recognizes it as a potential energy which can serve either the forces of rebellion or the angels of God. Angels do not perceive objects the same way we humans do; thus, a dollar bill, or money, is as unreal to the heavens as a painting of an apple (compared to a real apple) is here. When humans put money into motion, the attitude toward the object and its use is perceived by the heavens. It is important, therefore, that we focus on the way we transform the physical side of money into a spiritual energy force.

Our monetary system was originally connected to an awareness of God as the source of all, as indicated by the ancient symbol used on the dollar bill, the eye of God looking at us.

In the earlier stages of our monetary system, there was real gold to back each dollar bill. This is significant from a spiritual viewpoint. Gold is one of the rare substances that have a special connection with the heavens. Gold should be viewed as liquid sunlight which has congealed within the earth, and the light of the sun is connected to God. This is why ancient cultures used gold for religious figures, not for monetary value. We entered a situation earlier this century where our paper money ceased to be backed by gold bars. Such an event has serious spiritual implications. *We lost the connection with the spiritual sun force in our monetary system.* This opened the way for other influences to siphon off the energy which has operated as our money.

The solution is to replace the gold on a spiritual level. We can do this each time we make a monetary transaction. As you give a check, receive money from a cashier, or handle money directly, envision the light from the sun streaming into the storehouse for our gold located in Fort Knox, Kentucky. See the dollar bill connected with the sun. I also recommend that people say to themselves that the real gold lies within the heart of each person. Try this and you will see amazing things start to happen as you deal with money. Much of the fear and resistance and even attachment to it will be lifted, because your guardian angel will be responding to the images you are creating.

I have had to work continually with the process of monetary transformation and I have discovered some valuable results. If you approach money as a spiritual energy committed only for use by God, surprising things occur. First, I found that there were always enough resources available to do the work. The money might come in five minutes before midnight on the last day, but it is always there. I also learned that it was much better, if I gave someone money they needed, to require that they not repay the loan to me. I would always stipulate that they were not indebted to me but to God and had to share that same amount with other people in need. I think we can all give to others, no matter how little we think we have.

The next level in learning how to work with the angels in terms of money has to do with that nasty topic of who really owns everything and where your allegiance is given. Let's explore a sequence of thought that might explain this better. I will ask you: who do you work for? If you automatically name a specific company or even your own business, you may have a problem. I believe that there are only two employers in the world, no matter what the name of the corporation you might work for. One employer is yourself, operating under the influence of the forces of resistance. The other employer is God. You can say that, yes, you do wish to work for God. This does not mean becoming an instant missionary. It means that your focus will be clearer.

The next question that will arise is: who then pays you? If you work for God, then you are paid by God even if the check is signed with another name. It is impossible to work for God and not connect with the real source of monetary energy. Now another question arises. If you are paid by God and God is perfection, how can you be doing without unless you are refusing to receive heaven's paycheck? Each time you release money to pay bills, whose money are you using? If you view your money as God's energy, then payment of bills becomes easier, and the grip of materialism is loosened. Also, the ego gratification of having acquired more of God's energy than another person begins to have no meaning unless the money is used in service to help the angels and improve conditions for humanity.

As we begin to think on these things, we come close to an understanding of why people in so many parts of our world are undernourished. We are being asked by the angels to correct how we view nourishment on an economic and spiritual level. When we do this, the manifestation of physical malnourishment that is part of our group experience will begin to change.

Most of us do not know how to nourish ourselves let alone receive lasting nourishment from the heavens. Many times I have seen well-paid executives, spiritually aware executives, who are unable to maintain a balance between the demands of the materially oriented business world and their personal desire for spiritual harmony. I remember a trip that I took to New York City a few years ago. I observed the harshness of life reflected in the way people moved about from place to place. Faces were downcast, frozen into a determination to reach a destination without inconvenience or interaction with anyone. Despite the beauty of clothing and faces, there was an ugliness in the manner in which people interacted. I recall an incident when a woman rudely jolted me aside on the sidewalk so she could rush by. I readjusted my coat, which had been disarranged by the force of her blow, but kept walking in a graceful serene pace which is more in harmony with the movement of the angels. When I arrived at the corner to await the green traffic light, there was this same woman, huffing and spewing out vitriolic denunciation at the light. Her injury to me, which was not only a violation of my space but a real jarring to my spine, was totally unnecessary. She had not made any extra time by pushing me aside.

I think that such behavior is symptomatic of our times and relates to many levels of interaction other than how people move about in New York City. In business there is a tendency to push a competitor aside rather than to let the work stand on its own merits. In medicine, people may be pushed away from certain treatment centers because they don't have money or insurance. Such people are viewed as "not keeping up the pace," and it becomes acceptable to pass them by, ignoring the value of their lives. All of these types of negative actions are the result of insecurity. The person who rushes does not see things from a heavenly perspective, where everything is timed perfectly and thus there is no need to rush as long as one is in harmony with the Divine. The business that becomes more concerned with competition than with its own work quality operates on fear of loss.

If we are to understand the pathway to lasting spiritual nourishment that will lead to abundance on all levels, it is first necessary for us to view this from an angelic perspective. *God's love is the only lasting form of nourishing energy.* From the heavenly perspective, this love has always been and remains continuous. We live surrounded by it at all times even if we do not feel it or are not conscious of it. It is an illusion to think that spiritual nourishment means ingesting a dose of bliss as we would go to a gas station to refill our tank. Even prayer and meditation do not actually bring anything to us from the angels' viewpoint. Instead, we lift up barriers to our connection with this force of love.

This is an important point to understand. The angels are always around us; therefore, the emphasis is on remembering their presence. The same with the love of God. When we forget its presence it cannot be experienced. So, it is up to us to remember not only the presence of the angels but also that *the loving nourishment from God is constant* and always available when we develop a unified focus.

The implications of this view of nourishment are clear. When we feel insecure in our material world, we have chosen to place our faith in that very material world rather than to be sustained by the heavens. When we feel poor financially or empty emotionally, we have lost the connecting link to the love of God. It will be available as soon as we choose to reconnect.

Why do you think some souls choose paths of spiritual error such as lives of violence or crime? It is because they have lost faith in the wisdom and generosity of the Divine, frequently because they do not see results soon enough. The doubt of Godly abundance in their lives opens them up to negative influence that convinces them that they must take action to get what they want.

I once worked with a woman who had had a difficult childhood. She was raised as many people are without much financial or emotional security. As she developed through life, she became a person who found it important to acquire material possessions, as a sign that she was nourishing herself and doing well.

She was also a generous person with material objects. However, you could see that her identity was connected to the possessions she had accumulated. The time came when she had obtained all she could fit into her house. She had purchased cars and trips and baubles. With each passing year she became more unhappy inside and could not understand why. To the outer world she was very successful, but inside she was miserable. Her relationships deteriorated significantly. Her health began to fail, and she could no longer maintain the business she ran.

When I last saw this individual I knew that a crisis was ahead for her. The connection to God's love was not present in her consciousness. I could see that angelic lessons of true abundance were before her, and I prayed that the heavens would be merciful in the process of realigning her life. Sadly, the progression into misery continued. Finally the day arrived when circumstances brought her to the realization that her whole life had been spent chasing after power in the form of money and acquisitions. As she began to realign with God, she saw the truth of her life and the world she had created for herself. She commenced the slow process of prioritizing her spiritual life.

During her lifetime, she had used money for emotional security and it had crippled her. It was as if she had been leaning on a stick that was too short. Only by developing inner truth was she able to realign herself with God and become truly happy. There are millions of people like her in our world, and each one will suffer until he or she remembers the source of all that is lasting.

The angels cannot violate our choices. If we have chosen to disconnect from Divine abundance and rely only on material security, they will stand aside and hope that the experience will be beneficial to the spiritual growth of the human being they accompany through life.

Sometimes there are certain obstacles that we create in the path of receiving the real abundance of heaven. One of the most significant is resentment that things or events have not worked out the way we hoped or planned. The reason this is difficult for the angels is that our thinking has become fixed to a specific idea that has little to do with an awareness of the perfection of God's will.

An example of this is when a relationship breaks apart, as frequently happens in our society. One party seeks to make a change and the other one wants to remain as they were. This can be extremely painful for both parties but especially difficult for the one who is left. It is at such times that the temptation occurs to become resentful and even bitter. The person might feel that something has been taken away from his or her life, and it is hard to see that heaven has not stopped providing nourishment. At times like these, be aware that the angel has not failed in its duty to help nourish you through a relationship with another human being. There has only been a change in the type of relationship.

When we resent changes in our lives, it causes us to doubt the wisdom of our angel. This can make it difficult to recognize the new potentials coming that might be better in the long run. When we fixate on the loss rather than dwell on the wisdom of the angels, the pain can be more intense, and development of new relationships becomes more difficult.

Such a situation is comparable to the age-old saying about how our outlook on life depends upon whether we view our cup as half full or half empty. I think we need to realize that all abundance from the heavens is continually in motion. It is necessary for the energy to flow out, even overflow at times. Furthermore, it is very important that *when we can see only a few drops left, we remember that this means completely fresh waters of heaven will be coming to us soon.*

I can't stress enough how essential it is to give out, to find ways to nourish other people in our lives without expecting anything in return. There will always be plenty if we are connected to the realms of heaven where the true source of abundance exists. If we seek to collect material possessions, money, or power as security, or if we hold on to specific people in our lives for our main source of nourishment rather than depending upon the Creator to maintain us, we have entranced ourselves in illusion. Eventually, life will harden to the point where nothing will flow in any direction. Such a condition is to be consciously avoided.

To keep things fluid, each of us should discover what works best for our own situation so that we can continually receive angelic nourishment. The following are some suggestions that might be considered:

- If you find yourself having thoughts of lack on any level in your life, change the focus from "I don't have" to "I already have." You will be amazed at how your entire focus will change from the negative to the positive. Before long you will truly appreciate your life and its abundance. If you have to pay bills, instead of complaining about how little will be left afterward, be grateful that you had the resources to pay what you could. If you feel that you don't have enough people in your life, appreciate the ones who are there that you interact with, even if it is only the postal carrier or delivery person.

- From now on be active each day in tithing to God's angels, whether that involves money or energy. This means sharing some part of yourself with others for a selfless purpose. Traditionally, tithing was derived from farmers who would reserve 10 percent of the crop in one year for planting in the next. The laws of Moses stated that tithing was essential to a healthy spiritual life. This has led many people to share 10 percent of their money with their church, temple, or other worthy causes. What I suggest is that in addition one recognize that the angels of heaven have provided abundantly, even if it is not visible at the moment, and that *part of this blessing must be passed on to other souls.* To just write out a check would not be sufficient unless one made some personal connection or had some conscious involvement. The point is to spread the seeds of heaven into the world around us. For example, do not just donate money to a shelter for the homeless. Why not take time to connect with even one person? Perhaps you could arrange for someone to have a new suit of clothes so he or she could go on job interviews, or be given a day of cleansing and rest at a hotel, or something else appropriate. Homeless persons are not just drunken bums; they are people who need loving assistance. Money is not always the solution either; more important is a feeling that someone cares.

- Examine the definition you hold of abundance. If you see someone lacking in material possessions that you might have, visualize their angel bringing to them the riches of God, spiritually as well as materially. When seeing ostentatious wealth, create a picture in your mind of angels working with energy reserves, seeking to remind us to balance outer wealth with spiritual development. As you visualize someone destitute receiving an abundance from heaven in material form, also picture persons with extreme material wealth receiving spiritual balance commensurate with the material riches they have accumulated.

- Each morning upon rising, nourish your soul along with your body before or after breakfast. Set aside some time, even if only ten minutes, to pray for other people. Your angel is especially pleased when the day can start off this way. I suggest you pray for others, and, if you ask anything for yourself, that it be only that you become closer to God during the day. That is an excellent way to cover a multitude of personal problems. If you have a difficult business meeting ahead of you, spend this time to remember your guardian angel and ask that the angel establish a connection with the guardian angel of the other person. Do not ask your angel to convince the other person of what you want to achieve; instead, trust that your angel will strengthen the presence of the other person's angel. This will establish a potential for harmony based on what is best for all parties concerned.

- If you receive a gift from anyone, recognize that the angels participated in the process even if the human being who gave it to you was unaware. Acknowledge the person's generosity but also acknowledge your own guardian angel and the angel of the other person. If the gift does not make your heart dance with joy because it is not what you might provide for yourself, acknowledge the process that went on between you and the other person. The receiving of the energy behind a gift is more important than the item itself.

- Holiday meals should be a time for spiritual reflection while also dining. Many of these events become times of social warfare, which makes it difficult for the angels to stay in the same room. If people could only see that when we are eating, it is so important from the angels' view that there be serenity, which will enable heavenly processes to assist with the activity of digestion. All meals should become times when we recognize that a holy event is transpiring even if we don't understand it. The very least we can do is to think of spiritual topics when actually eating.

- If there is anything in your life to which you feel particularly attached, such as a certain house, job, car, piece of jewelry, artwork, furniture, memorabilia, let go of it in your mind. Having the object is not an obstacle unless there is attachment to it. If you don't release yourself from material connections while alive, it becomes more difficult to shed these desires after death. Be *willing* to separate yourself from any possessions you have immediately, if that is the will of God.

- If you are feeling ill and experiencing the weakness frequently associated with poor health, it is a sign that it is time to focus on balancing all the levels on which you receive nourishment, from physical to spiritual. Each time you go to sleep, prepare yourself by asking God to bring balance to your life. The angel will witness this request and help in delivery of the response according to the will of God.

When important national events occur, it is a time to remind yourself that our nation has an archangel who cares for us in the same way that the guardian angel is responsible for an individual soul. Ask your angel to relay to God a request that your angel be permitted to help the archangel of the nation to align with the will of God. When traveling to other nations or hearing about international events, remember to picture the participation of the archangels overseeing each part of the world. If we would all respond to the promptings of the guardian angels, who in turn would be in harmony with the archangels, we could solve many of the global issues that threaten us.

A REMINDER FROM HEAVEN

There is one realization that the angels know would be good for us to have in our consciousness. It has to do with the Angels' Cup. This image means that when we are connected to Divine love, we are drinking from the Cup of Heaven. What makes this cup special is that it never runs out of the offering, with one exception: if we do not share the energy of the Divine but attempt to block it off for ourselves alone, we will find the cup has been emptied. The secret of keeping the cup brimming with energy is to give to others without thought of self. If we choose to nourish others in selfless ways, the angels of heaven will be sure to maintain our own connection to Divine nourishment. All that we could ever need will be provided.

Chapter Seven

HEAVEN IS KNOCKING! OPEN THE DOOR!

If we are to avoid the imminent abyss we face, it is essential that we learn to make the right choices starting immediately. This requires taking personal responsibility for our lives and our role in society. The heavens are asking all humanity to realign priorities and help the emissaries of God to overcome the crisis that faces our civilization.

For starters, we can begin to fulfill these requests from the heavens:

STUDY CELESTIAL REALMS

We should know that it is only while we are on earth that we can gain conscious learning about the workings of the spiritual world. When we die, we bring with us into the realms of heaven the deeds of our lives as well as the amount of learning we gained about the spiritual realms while alive. If one has chosen not to study the heavens before death, one cannot do it when in those realms after death.

For those who actually study the angelic hierarchies and cosmology that includes planetary spheres, and, in addition, do active work on moral transformation, the experience after death is vastly improved. Through these efforts a person becomes conscious of the angelic realms in such a way that the angels can more easily lift his or her soul after death. These types of thoughts held during life will also permit the guardian angel, upon the death of the human, to lead the soul into greater realms of spiritual light than normally would be possible.

It works somewhat like this: if your guardian angel knows that you have studied the celestial realms, you will receive a special welcome when passing through the death process. For example, if you were invited to a dinner party with a group of opera singers and you had prepared yourself by learning about opera, composers, singers, and music, the people with whom you dined would be able to speak with you and develop personal relationships. The same is true in the realms of heaven. If you avoid this study, it is like arriving at the dinner party not even knowing what opera was or how to eat at a dinner table.

Serious study of the realms of heaven enables one to be in the presence of very pure spiritual beings because one will have been prepared. The angels that greet one in the realms of heaven will be waiting to receive from each soul the results of spiritual knowledge. If very little has been obtained through the thinking capacity, then very little is offered to the angels. Such a lack has great impact on limitations in future lives.

EXAMINE THE COSMIC VIEW

Learn about Christ, Buddha, or any of the prophets from a cosmological as well as religious viewpoint. See their actions and impact on civilization from the perspective of heaven, not as we humans interpret things. Become aware of how much our religions interpret history in very materialistic ways. Seek to discover the participation of the angels in terms of the development of our civilization. You can begin this study by supplementing traditional sacred texts with the works of other writers who have sought to explain spiritual mysteries throughout the centuries. Read them with an open mind even if you find what they say is in opposition to your particular religion. Once you become aware of the vastness of material on this subject, you can begin to focus on particular areas of interest. Seek to locate material that includes humanity's relationship to the sun and discusses the connection between the Creator and the formation of the solar system. As you examine these writings, you will discover that many of *the great secrets of the workings of heaven are disguised in symbol to protect against misuse of knowledge.* This has resulted in religious history being interpreted in very limited and literal ways as opposed to the actual meaning.

If you seriously approach the discovery of truth behind ancient events, your angel will help. This being, who is connected to the Source, knows the truth or can obtain it for you.

Be open to explore the works of various writers, from philosophers to theologians to individuals who have had direct experience with the realms of heaven.

EXPAND COSMIC MEMORY

It is time to develop our cosmic memory. Some persons have already opened spiritual organs that are for this purpose, but they do not have any actual memories because of lack of cognitive abilities in earlier times. There can be no memory without cognition. With organs open to work with cosmic memory and no actual memories, a person can develop a painful nervous condition, somewhat analogous to the problems experienced in the past few years by persons who are environmentally sensitive to almost all substances.

We should begin to develop our spiritual memory by being fully awake in any activity other than actual sleep, and by becoming active inwardly in these experiences.

APPLY YOUR SPIRITUAL KNOWLEDGE

There are all types of knowledge about spiritual topics available to humanity and a lot of confusion about their differences. True spiritual knowledge is close to wisdom in that there must be some experience involved. In this sense, spiritual knowledge means a conscious study of the workings of heavenly spheres, the angelic hierarchies, the teachings of the prophets and saints, and the relationship of Divine law to the development of human life. Ideally, the attainment of spiritual knowledge should be a lifelong pursuit; however, each of us has some area of our lives where small bits of truth about God and our relationship to the Creator can receive our focus.

All persons should apply and fully use whatever

spiritual knowledge they possess; otherwise, this knowledge reverts to the use of adversary angels. Often this occurs on an unconscious basis. We have heard of the importance of utilizing heavenly gifts or talents; it is time to realize that lack of application of spiritual knowledge is on the same level as misuse of knowledge for personal gain.

RECOGNIZE THE WORKS OF HEAVEN

Redefine who should be valued as a great soul. Be ever aware that the persons who are great souls from heaven's viewpoint might not be recognized as such on earth. This is because they have no need for recognition. They need only to achieve their goals. In addition, they rarely comply with the packaging that society creates since it is materially oriented. Such souls are involved in teaching and therefore are working to help people overcome illusions. The days of celebrity worship based on money, power, beauty, or the ability to entertain will fade. The new way will be to let the strength of one's deeds indicate who is truly a great personality. If public personalities begin to demonstrate spiritual deeds along with the glitter of publicity, then their careers will be long-lasting. As you begin to recognize the presence of Divine impulses in the world around you, some very interesting things begin to happen. A good way to describe this situation would be the following image: Let us suppose you traveled down a road that had new and beautiful strips of flower beds planted along the roadway. If you were thinking about how much traffic there was or how your car was not behaving properly or why the driver in front seemed to take up the whole road, you would not even see the flowers. However, if you were inwardly still, despite the traffic and other problems, the flowers would catch your eye. Now let us suppose in the midst of the flower strip you saw a radiant angel hovering above the flowers. You would continue on your way, but each time you drove down a road that had flowers, you would look to see if you could spot another angel. What happens is that once we identify certain actions in the world that are inspired from the heavens, we actively seek to locate them everywhere. With each new discovery one's faith in the powers of goodness grows.

In terms of identifying people who are truly working for the heavens, the best way is to see the wave of energy they leave behind. Such people can be described as being similar to a meteor, blazing through life and leaving behind a trail of light. These beings who work for the heavens prefer the angelic form of recognition, which is to have their message heeded rather than to be honored.

BE DISCERNING

Be extremely cautious about accepting any "channeling" process because it causes the consciousness to be divided. The information received is unlikely to be valid despite how appealing it is to the human ego. The reason one cannot depend upon such material is that the receiver must, by the nature of the process involved, dim his or her own consciousness for the channeling to occur. There are various levels to this dimming. In extreme cases it can lead to full possession of the body by the soul imparting the information.

There are various problems with this activity. First, the human beings who have agreed to dim their consciousness for the procedure have not united their own souls with the experience. In order for an imprint upon one's soul forces to occur, memory must be involved. Memory requires consciousness.

Another problem is that the astral realm that surrounds the earth is swarming with souls who for one reason or another have not been lifted into the realms of heavenly spheres after death. Such souls are frequently overly attached to the earth and are also very limited in moral development prior to death. They associate with humans who seek to communicate with the spiritual world through such methods as channeling, even when the intention is to harmlessly communicate with one's own angel. However, guardian angels do not need to dim the consciousness of humans. They can inspire directly through the mind without taking over anyone's body, even for a short period of time. The same caution applies to automatic writing or other psychic games and activities. They are very dangerous because the earthbound disincarnated souls can seem to give brilliant and partially true information to whet your appetite; however, they can eventually take over the body completely and permanently. In the old days, including biblical times, this was referred to as being possessed. Imbalances in relating to the outer world occur, as well as major interference between the true guardian angel and the new trespasser. The disharmony can lead to various forms of mental illness.

The other threat has to do with the fact that it is of great interest to the rebellious angels whenever a person seeks to channel information. It is like an open door to them, allowing these beings to provide very tricky information that may seem to be harmless on the surface. However, the effect of the transmitted material is to mislead and to incite egotism and greed. Also, when the person starts to "channel" information, he or she begins to refer to the source of the material as different from the self and therefore an authority that cannot be challenged. In addition, the person allowing his or her body to be used does not acknowledge responsibility for the material given.

One should not minimize the danger of channeling no matter how glorious the material relayed seems to be. Eventually the level will degrade, and the hidden intention of the rebellious angel, or disincarnated spirit, will show itself. A clue to watch for is the increasing dependence of listeners upon the source of information.

With all this said, I must clarify that there have been a handful of rare exceptions this century wherein the information received under dimmed consciousness was effective in relieving the physical imbalances of other people. On those extremely rare occasions, a prebirth agreement existed for the soul to bring certain types of spiritual knowledge into the world in this way. This was due to limitations of the current personality which could not permit a conscious interaction.

The old way of channeling must give way to new

methods of true, soundly based, inspiration and intuition. The difference between these modes can be viewed like this: in ancient times the personality had to be dimmed to prevent interference with Divine guidance, and thus the process was much like raising the arms to heaven to receive. At this point in our planetary development, we need to form our consciousness, our thinking, feeling, and willing parts, into a transformed vehicle that can give us direct access to the heavens. We expand our consciousness, but we do not lose it or dim it. Through this expansion *that results only from transformation of the soul and personality*, the person can directly experience the truths of heaven. Thus, illusions do not occur, because one is protected by the angelic hierarchies as well as the amount of light that one radiates.

If you seek to share with humanity knowledge about the spiritual world, the only way your consciousness can be lifted into the realms of heaven is through the power of your accomplished deeds in the outer world combined with a willingness to undergo moral transformation. *One cannot enter the realms of light without having a substantial amount of light oneself.* True knowledge of the spiritual world is possible only by lifting, with the help of the angels, an expanded consciousness into those realms in a selfless, yet focused, manner.

The pathway that involves accepting other disincarnated souls into oneself was practical in ancient times. However, it is *not* endorsed by the good forces of heaven any longer because of the way it encourages human attachment to lower energies. The direction now used by the heavens involves individuals being lifted in their own consciousness into heavenly realms *through the power of their deeds in the outer world and by the will to undergo moral transformation.*

There is a contagion of people seeking to communicate with angels by channeling. This is totally unnecessary because angels have been working *directly* through human consciousness since the beginning of existence. It is up to us whether we work with the angels of God or with the rebellious ones. The *safe* way is built on humility, clarity, and real knowledge of the workings of heaven that involves the use of true inspiration. Remember the inspiration that motivated Leonardo da Vinci and others of his caliber. They were conscious and did not "channel," but allowed their deeds to reflect the heavens.

IDENTIFY UNTRUTHS

Work every day to be free from the lies of our era produced by the spirits of falsehood. We are immersed in them, from product advertising to all areas of life. When people want to deny that a lie is involved, they will develop a memory problem. Many false memories are therefore being imbedded in our etheric body through the way we live. This hinders the help of Archangel Michael. When you see a falsehood do not become aggressive but clear the way between others and yourself. If you want to remove untruths that you have accepted within you, keep a list of the little things you say that are not true. Work either to make them true or to stop telling the falsehoods. *Be secure in the knowledge that the truth of who you are is what God and his angels want at all times.* Because of the present condition of our civilization, there is a probability that persons who deny the reality of heaven will not like you. Give them time, and remember that they, too, are your spiritual relatives even though they do not recognize you.

DON'T COMPROMISE TRUTH

Develop an unwavering dedication to the truth—to live it, to speak it, to identify it, to defend it in all ways. However, *never impose your truth on another person.*

One of the most common responses is that everyone sees truth differently. Yes, this is so while we are in physical form. But in the realms of heaven there are no variations, only harmony. For example, the wisdom of Buddha still exists and if followed is very helpful. The teachings of Jesus Christ are filled with love and can help a person change his or her whole way of life. Both sources are providing true information. Even though they seem different on the earth, in the angelic realms they are *both* stating a truth, and there is harmony between these streams in heaven.

The point here is that when you discover a heavenly truth, be loyal to it. However, do not violate the rights of another person by demanding that they accept the truth you have discovered.

As you read the pages of this book, know there is a preset acknowledgment in my mind that you may disagree with me on some things. I have no interest in trying to convince you that your opinion would be wrong. Sometimes the very process of discovering dif-

ferent versions of truth leads one to deep spiritual
growth. If I argued that this book was the only book
for you to read and that in order to work with the
angels you must not question anything, it would be directly opposed to the intentions of the angels. However, I will maintain a loyalty to the truth as it has
been experienced by me. This does not mean you will
have the same experience of truth.

*Never relinquish an experience of truth for the sake
of approval by others.*

ELIMINATE JUDGMENT

It is important to develop the ability to identify
the various illusions and temptations to which you are
susceptible, but without any judgment of yourself or
others. Instead, arrive at this awareness with *love.*
Whenever you have discerned that illusions or temptations may be involved in the actions or life of another,
check yourself to see if you have judged that person.
Judgment involves the element of condemnation. Ask
yourself if you would be willing to help the person if
they were in need and came to you for assistance. If
you can picture yourself helping them without hesita-
tion, then it is likely that dangerous judgment has not
been exercised. Rather, loving discernment has been
utilized for the purpose of spiritual knowledge.

Remember that as soon as one makes a judgment,
even if justified as part of religious practice, one has
stolen from the heavens. This seems very strong, but if
you realize that the only judgment permitted in the
universe originates with God alone, it is clear that
when we act as though we have the right to judge an-

other, we have presumed an authority that belongs to the Creator. Judgment from God relies upon spiritual laws and our soul development. It never incorporates condemnation, which is the opposite of love. When we humans condemn others, the quality of healthy discernment has become polluted with negative influence that will prevent the angels from supporting our action. Whenever we put up an energy wall of intolerance, the angels experience the same barrier. Sadly, those very judgments will return to the person who released them, frequently on a more difficult level.

How this occurs is very interesting. After one withdraws from the physical body at death and enters the spiritual world, there is a period of experience when one directly faces the very judgments he or she placed on other people during life. This can be a very painful process if, for example, one has judged other people falsely. Those same reasons that justified the judgment are shone on one's past life with the help of the angel. This experience causes you to directly feel the same force of condemnation that you gave out to others. This reflective process is one of the ways angels work to help humanity turn from patterns of negative behavior. Conversely, if you are truly loving to other people during life, you will experience this same feeling and attitude reflected back to you.

It is important to explain the subject of forgiveness. If one has changed his or her life, ceased judgments, and been forgiven by self and the Divine, the review process is somewhat different. The behavior before the change is relived, but as a distant memory, much as recalling a painful visit to the dentist is different from actually reliving it. Events in life that occur after forgiveness will not have the stinging element of judgment present but instead will have the comfortable experience of acceptance.

A wonderful way to overcome the tendency to judge others is to hold the belief that you never truly know another person. Perhaps, despite appearances or actions, you might be condemning a messenger from heaven. We have all been told for many thousands of years to remember that within each person God also dwells.

Be Humble

Humility is one of the most important attitudes of soul. If anyone does not humble himself or herself before the angels of God and the heavens, the responsibility falls to the guardian angel to teach the soul the meaning of this spiritual quality. This means that if the person has misused his or her free will to the point where arrogant behavior has appeared and pride is worn as an outer garment, the lesson will be taught by Divine law, which will severely limit the person's independence, perhaps through illness or in social interaction. To work with the heavens requires an inner nature that is modest, courteous to those of greater wisdom, and able to recognize levels of importance. This does not mean going about with an attitude of weakness or even outwardly displaying the role of a humble one. On the contrary, the heavens celebrate a soul with strength that can inspire others and also maintain an inward attitude of being able to humble oneself before God.

I find that in the spiritual field there are so many gifted people. Frequently I find these gifts surrounded with a coating of pride in self or an overvaluing of the work one does. It has become important for me to maintain a level of humility over the years. On occasion, the heavens provide an opportunity for a refresher course on what is really important in our offerings. One such event happened when I was doing a workshop in California. I was giving a lecture on overcoming obstacles and being oneself when one of my front tooth caps clattered onto the table in front of me.

I was horrified, but the group asked me to keep talking, so I continued throughout the day helping them to become free of limitations in their lives. I was embarrassed at first, but at the end of the day many people came up to me and told me that the incident had helped drive home the very message I had been trying to deliver. That day I learned the necessity of humility while performing the work of the heavens. It was wonderful for me to realize that my situation became an instrument for the angels.

Whenever you find yourself in an embarrassing position, use it as a reminder of the need to balance your life with humility. As you achieve greater and greater skills in the name of God, you will feel a deep inner pull to place yourself on your knees before the greatness of heaven.

AVOID TYRANNY

Be alert to whether you have allowed yourself to be under the will of another person or group of persons or if you have put other humans under your own will. This applies to work, family, and even friends. Sometimes the influence is very subtle; at other times it can be as strong as peer pressure among teenagers or believing that as adults we cannot say "no" to group mind images that are programming us from the entertainment and media world. This group influence can also happen in business.

An example would be if you are working for a company that you don't believe in, even though you might be receiving remuneration that you like. The company has purchased you, and unless you are in harmony with what the company is seeking to do and how it is going about achieving the goal, you will eventually wear out in this situation. In terms of family, if you have a mate whose will you operate under, the moment eventually arrives when the weight of the shackles becomes too great, and the relationship shatters as you reach for inner freedom. The same applies to friendships and other areas of our lives.

Sometimes this experience of being under another's will is disguised as one person lovingly serving another, but this actually is rarely so. Instead, it is a situation where one party has relinquished his or her life to control by another. Such a condition is difficult for the angels to work with until the parties involved balance out will influences.

Avoid the Desire Trap

Learn to develop nonpersonal wishes. This also helps in the workings of Michael because it releases us from certain hindrances that work through our desires no matter how good they may be. If we can develop nonpersonal desires, such as "I hope everyone can experience the love of God through their angel" rather than "I want to feel my angel *right now*," we will be on the right path.

Our society is filled with the belief that desires are healthy and good. Some are, but most of them hide the secret maneuverings of the rebellious forces in our lives. Even spiritually minded people can be detoured on their path by the desire nature. For example, the desire to help others is certainly laudable, but it can be subtly manipulated by angels opposed to God. This can lead to many unnecessary disappointments and problems. If you would like to help others, decide to do it with a foundation of good thinking combined with balanced action. *Avoid desire being the motive, and your work will be more successful and truly beneficial.*

PURIFY LANGUAGE

Use language in a *sacred manner*, as it was intended, for communication. Avoid untruthful communication and the use of spoken or written words to distort spiritual truths for religious empowerment. Words should not be tools for support of prejudicial acts, including gossip. Become aware of how much of the media is based on gossip and involves flagrant misuse of words. Every time we gossip, we fill our souls with pollution.

Newspapers, magazines, and television shows that sensationalize human difficulties and deliberately manipulate the viewer or reader by shock methods are

tter than advertisements from hell with a little
rown in. The seduction from these offerings is
very real and addictive. The worst part of their existence is their profit from the suffering or mistakes of
people, and they feel it is their right to invade the privacy of anyone and everyone. Tabloid journalism is focused on competing for a story rather than seeking the
truth.

Be discerning about whatever you hear or read
from this type of journalism. Avoid reading or listening to material that awakens your tendency to judge
others, creates feelings of avarice and jealousy, or seems
to *invade the right of privacy of any person.* This misuse
of language can only be stopped if the society in which
it has been accepted supports it no longer.

Be advised that it is almost painful for guardian
angels when people gossip about one another—in of-
fices, hospitals, schools, churches, or anyplace where
this occurs. When people say unpleasant things about
others for the pleasure of sharing the experience, an
awful thing occurs on a spiritual level. Along with the
negative words, little serpent figures creep out of the
mouth of the speaker. From a heavenly viewpoint, it
is a very ugly sight that repels the angels.

If you are in the midst of people who thrive on
gossip, you have an obligation to refuse to participate
if you wish to be connected to the angels of God.
However, to force others to stop gossiping would be a
violation. You can withdraw from the gathering or an-
nounce that you do not wish to gossip. Try to suggest
a positive thought or idea or a subject that might
pique their interest and change the energy.

Spiritually minded people should pay very close attention to this. *When words are used to harm another, one is committing a crime against heaven.* This is the reason for the old statement we heard as children, "If you can't think of something nice [and true] to say about someone, don't say anything." The only exception is one of those occasions when knowledge one has might prevent unnecessary pain for another. Then one can tell the news, but in a compassionate way.

Another aspect to the language pollution problem is that there is no longer any respect for privacy. Addiction to sensational news makes journalists accept no boundary for stories they will air or publish. The lack of respect shown for one another all around the world shows up in the unwillingness to let people have their private lives and personal thoughts. It is as if anyone the media wish to write about, speak about, or interview becomes the personal property of the journalists—someone with whom they can do whatever they want to enhance circulation or ratings. Yes, there are journalists who are not part of this group. They are the golden ones whose sense of truth radiates from their work. Sadly, there are too few in our present world.

There is nothing that seems to be recognized as sacred or off limits anymore in terms of news. The media have become so extreme that I wonder if the day will come when someone reports on how the Pope or the President practices personal hygiene. It is time to change our focus and be more balanced.

I am reminded of how this imbalance surfaced in a recent event involving a celebrity who sustained a life-threatening injury. The international press besieged the town and the hospital, literally camping out. They not only wanted medical reports, but also photographs of him in the midst of his suffering. Fortunately, this insensitive behavior was contained by those in charge of his care.

Be clear with your words, be truthful, and let the energy of God purify your speech and communications on all levels.

LIFT YOUR CONSCIOUSNESS

Even though we feel that our lives are often out of control due to time schedules and demands, the angels would like us to be aware of those moments when our thinking has become bound by the world and lift these thoughts to a heavenly perspective. It will help in revealing the truth of a situation and will give strength in completing tasks. If you spend more time thinking about your job or your clothes or your illness or your problems than you devote to God, then you are not free to move with the angels.

Suppose you find yourself having to complete a project for work that takes all your attention. Delays occur that were unexpected and pressure mounts. How will you lift your consciousness in such a situation? Remember that your guardian angel is right beside you in the office or job and will help you complete the task *provided you carry your spiritual consciousness into your work*. This does not mean publicly proclaiming your relationship to God, but it *does* mean recognizing that you have the help of the heavens even in the midst of completing a difficult business report under pressure. You will find that if you remember the presence of the angels, the tasks become easier and are completed in half the time.

Whenever you are confronted with difficult tasks that add stress to life, allow for the help of your angel to reduce this stress. The angel will assist as long as you maintain your focus on the important, lasting relationship to God.

BEGIN THE DETACHMENT PROCESS

It is time to practice real love that does not involve any attachment whatsoever. This does not eliminate commitment or responsibility; rather it allows for complete respect for freedom at any point in a relationship. Such an attitude will not lead to a breakdown in society. It will provide for the experience of true security, which is never based on another person but rather is based on the knowledge that God is truly the source of all love and all we would ever need if we could only identify it.

A healthy relationship can be compared to the meeting of two birds in flight. If the two people were to focus on each other rather than on God, their wings—figuratively speaking—would be so intertwined that neither could fly. If, however, they both focus on God as the birds should focus on sky, wind, and sun, they can fly together to all parts of the world.

So many times we allow fear to erase the potentials of our relationships. The fear of loss strangles the potentials and prevents a positive future, just as if one bird prevented the other bird from flying. We must remain free and enable others to stay free in all areas of their lives. This does not mean lack of involvement, or irresponsibility; it means focusing on the relationship in a healthy way.

I once met a couple that personified this quality in their relationship. The nature of both their careers required substantial travel. During a conversation with them someone asked how each of them could trust the other to be faithful in a world of so many temptations. They looked at each other, smiled, and answered, "That which God arranges we should never surround with fear." They had been together in this trusting manner for fifteen years and were exquisitely happy. Nor did they neglect the relationship, because they both knew that God was the center of their union. They described their life together as a huge tent with a great white pole in the center that supported everything and determined the space in which they would move. This pole was their combined love of God. As long as they both made sure the pole was in the right place, they were protected, and each person could breathe. If they focused too much on each other or looked to the other for inner support, they would turn their backs on the pole. Eventually, adjustments that should have been made would not be made, and the tent would fall down, suffocating both persons. This is also an image they used to explain freedom within a family unit. Such detachment does not imply irresponsibility or lack of commitment.

Love that has any attachments based on fear or ownership is not real love and will surely end a relationship in time. Like the old image of the butterfly in the open hand, true love requires freedom to take flight and the opportunity to remain by choice. If one closes the hand over the butterfly to hold it forever, it will only die.

There is one other image that helps to understand the importance of detachment. It is a statement I have made for many years to individuals who fear the loss of a relationship of some sort. *What God wills to remain in your life, you cannot get rid of no matter how hard you try.* Why hold on to something or someone that God may not want in your life?

Instead, seek to love everyone without attachment or fear of loss. Honor commitments, but build the relationship upon trust and respect for freedom.

AVOID BEING COMPETITIVE

Refuse to compete with anyone in your thinking and in your deeds, especially contests involving a judgment of who is best at something. Instead, strive for self-improvement and inner recognition of self as well as experiencing the presence of God within. The process of seeking to surpass others for personal gain is not part of a path to heaven and deters the angels of God from helping as they would like.

If you seek to measure your success by distancing yourself from others, the rebellious angels are involved in the activity. People mistakenly believe that achieving excellence requires defeating another person. This is illusion and has much to do with circumstances and such things as karmic law. *The real winner may excel over others, but his or her focus is only on improving a personal record.*

One of the main motivators for a feeling of com-

petition is lack of inner security. The way to overcome
such a limited attitude is by placing trust in your connection with God. This God force within you does
not need to compete with others. It can never be
shortchanged or lacking in what is real.

The other impulse behind competition is ego
gratification. Both insecurity and ego gratification are
products of the rebellious angels and will cause one to
become addicted to competition while depriving one
of a lasting joy in accomplishment.

We need to rethink competitive events and see
how they can be improved spiritually. It would be possible even for horse races to be run by the clock, as are
certain ski events. Many sports are already based on
personal best. Now it is time to avoid the negative aspect of competition in order to free ourselves from undue influences from the underworld on many levels.
We need to realize that in the business world it is an
illusion to think we must compete in the cutthroat
manner that has been accepted as essential for economic success. Capitalism can be practiced with a clear
spiritual perspective instead of being permeated with
the rancid smoke of competition.

Remember that the angels of God never compete
with one another or between the various levels of angelic hierarchies. A guardian angel working day by day
with a human being would never compare the value of
its work with that of the seraphim who are closest to
the Trinity. The seraphim would equally value the
work of the guardian angel. Each and every member of
creation asks *itself* how it has progressed on the pathway toward God.

DON'T JUSTIFY GREED

Likewise refuse to participate in or endorse gambling for personal gain. This business is encroaching on society each year under various guises intended to make it acceptable. The danger is that gambling opens one to negative influences that control false hope while encouraging greed.

Many spiritual people justify keeping gambling money because they will "use it to help others." This is poisonous money that will never create any lasting spiritual goodness. If you are truly willing to give away your winnings, then you will also know that there are better ways to raise money to help others despite how appealing the packaged idea. If you have an urge to bet on something, do it without money or personal gain being involved. If it is the thrill of the unexpected that you want to experience, go for a ride down country roads where you have never driven before and explore new sights or learn something new.

Gambling has a lot to do with control, tempting the person who gambles to believe he or she is going to win (be in control), while at the same time that person is becoming a prisoner of greed. Don't fool yourself by thinking you can just play in this area. Your playmates will be none other than the rebellious angels with their familiar offerings.

RELEASE THE NEED FOR PAIN

Awaken to how much of life is connected to addiction to pain. An example, other than the usual physical pain experiences, would be that we seem to need to bombard ourselves with increasing stress and shocking events in order to feel anything. Our society is becoming numb to the point where only the most extreme circumstances get our attention, and even then it is rare that change is made. We also expect others to create feelings in us rather than connecting with our own soul forces. This happens in relationships as well as through television, cinema, and now the media operating on sensationalism.

IDENTIFY YOUR REAL FAMILY

Work consciously to overcome influences that come from blood ties that can work against inner freedom. This does not mean to give up connections to relatives but rather to become conscious of group thinking, even ancestral thinking, and how it has formed your life. The angels need us to be completely free to recognize the new bonds of the spirit that will be introduced throughout our lives. Your birth family or marital family might also be your spiritual family. If it isn't, the angels will need you to be open to developing new relationships.

It is possible to recognize these new spiritual family members by the ease with which we can communicate. There is almost a silent recognition that is prepacked with respect for one another. Frequently, there is an unusual delight in knowing that the other person is on the earth. At the same time we do not seek to place any demands on this person. Freedom in the relationship is automatic and does not have to be learned. There are also similarities in perspective that often amaze both parties.

I find that when I am unable to be in contact

with one of my spiritual family members, there is no loss felt. When we do join together in conversation, it is as if we had put the last interaction on a hold button and knew right where we were. The reason this happens is that there truly is a familiarity of soul that originates in the spiritual world and creates a high level of intuitive understanding.

If you question whether someone in your life is part of your real spiritual family, that person probably is not, *because of the uncertainty.* If he or she is truly a spiritual family member, you would not even wonder. You would know right down to your bones. However, even though the person might not be a spiritual family member, he or she could be an important part of your inner growth, and thus you feel a strong connection. Remember, the real heavenly family members do not awaken feelings of attachment, desire, or dependency.

Sadly, one of the reasons people experience intense loneliness is that they have been unable to connect with those spiritual family members. When this connection happens, the power of recognition is quite nurturing and sustaining for both parties on the soul level. It can be likened to recognizing old classmates in a foreign country where you never expected to meet them. There is delight and appreciation. You visit, and then continue on the spiritual path each one has chosen.

CREATE ONLY SELFLESSLY

All creative deeds should involve thinking, feeling, and willing and, above all, should be done on behalf of the heavens, not ourselves. If you were to interview any of the great composers of the past, such as Beethoven, he would never say he composed music for himself. He was fulfilling a selfless mission to manifest the will of God through the impulse to create. *All truly creative deeds that will last upon the earth need to be done to honor the Creator.*

An example of the role of selflessness in creation of anything important has its archetype in the process of human birth. There would not be life if the mother's body did not give of its own substance for creation of the child.

To do something that is unique or different is not the kind of creativity that the heavens seek. The angels need us to connect whatever we create *to the Creator.* To do this, there are components that will lead to a creative result that is in harmony with the Divine: a level of truth, beauty, and goodness intentionally portrayed in the work product.

Whenever music, painting, or any other art form becomes only an extension of personal ego, it is difficult for the angels of God to be involved. Due to the absence of the angels of light, who are attracted only by works reflecting truth, beauty, and goodness, the door is opened to manipulation by the rebellious angels. Not only is the negative energy of these works discernible to persons connected to the angels of God, but upon observing the lives of such creators more closely you will discover a tendency to compete or to be manipulated by others.

This happens because the originator of the work became immersed in self or in materialism. *Everything one makes should be created for the glory of God,* no matter how small or how grand.

For years, I have on occasion taught people how to expand their creativity. We can all widen our service area for the heavens. Time and again, students discovered that when they stepped aside from an idea of what *they* wanted to create, and focused on Divine subjects, exquisite works would come flowing through their artform.

EXPAND YOUR FAITH

Faith should be developed out of free will, not as a result of traditional family or group enticement. Choice in the pathway to God must be completely one's own. So many families, communities, and even nations have been destroyed because people allowed undue religious influence. We have got to expand our faith as individuals but separate it from coercion. Connected to this is the extreme crisis that must be faced: the need for our civilization to cease condemning others of differing religious views, both within the different religions and between the religious paths.

This area has become the most successful campaign of the fallen angels: they wait until one has dedicated himself or herself to a particular path and is convinced of having the only pathway to God that is the right one. Soon to follow is the *judgment against others who are not part of that religion.* The heavens weep when this occurs, because so often the soul has been quite sincere in seeking a closer connection to God but chooses the adversaries at the very last minute, when judgment on a religious basis is used for strengthening the soul's own beliefs. This has been the root cause of most of the wars and devastation on our planet since humanity began to find different ways to honor God.

Once you have decided upon the specific devotional method, turn to it regularly, but do not demand that everyone around you do the same. Many marriages have been destroyed over religious and spiritual differences. Even if you pray at home, plan different occasions when you can join others in prayer, in a church, a temple, or even out in a meadow. The importance of religion is that it provides a structure to support time for prayer. It gives an opportunity to remind ourselves of a better way to live each day as well as a time to enjoy the company of others who love God. Even if we feel that our emphasis is personal spiritual work rather than religious, and that "church is within," it is still important to support gatherings in the name of God, no matter what religion or denomination. These institutions are the result of how the participants act, not the reverse. Do not walk away from anything that was created by God even if you do not understand it or do not agree.

I knew a woman many years ago who learned this lesson about harmony among religions as a component of a healthy faith. She lived in a major city in which there were many beautiful churches. Although she was quite happy being of the Jewish faith, she realized that Archangel Michael was recognized not only in her religion but also in the Catholic religion. She began a pilgrimage all over the city into every church or place of holy worship in order to share the common faith in God. I might add that she found an amazing way to fit into these different houses of God. Her attitude of enthusiastic openness to different faiths caused the people she encountered to assume she was a part of their community, and they welcomed her to all their activities. This time of expansion of faith had a great impact on her life. Often she has spoken of the many little miracles she experienced during her pilgrimage.

One of my favorite images that personifies this joining together in the name of God has to do with a cathedral in Paris called Sacre Coeur, or Sacred Heart. It was created to honor the universality of all peoples, and what I experienced there was magnificent. As I walked up the steps of the beautiful white building, I noticed an unusual amount of angels of all levels. I heard the sounds of a choir singing with the clarity of bells. It was just prior to a mass or service, and the cathedral was filled with people. Stunned, I quietly walked around the outer chambers of the cathedral. Everywhere people were in the postures of the different religions. Moslems were prostrate on their prayer rugs; Catholics had their rosaries; Buddhists were quietly seated in the lotus position, chanting; Jews were wearing their sacred garments and reading prayers from the Old Testament. People of other religions were there, too. I observed this exquisite sight with tears streaming down my cheeks. I realized why the angels were gathering in this truly sacred place that day. It was because of the open heart of the people.

Many people have difficulty in this area of expanding their faith because of the disappointments they have experienced or the ugliness and suffering in the world. In terms of personal events that have occurred in the past, look back over them with the perspective of heaven. Seek to discover the new strengths that you experienced, the new opportunities and new growth that were linked to any unpleasant events. For example, think of the amount of compassion that is awakened in humanity with any terrible tragedy such as an earthquake or hurricane. Is it not possible that those individuals who died had completed their work on earth, and the means of their death became a heavenly instrument to create new levels of compassion? *Remember, compassion is a critical door opener to help from the heavens.* Whenever we are kind and giving to one another, this attracts the interest and aid of angels in a tremendous way.

If possible, each day look over events from a higher perspective. When this is done with frequency, a pattern begins to emerge showing that God is very involved in our lives in ways we rarely discover. What appears to be a loss or difficulty also brings with it a blessing that should be discovered. Whenever one has a shortage of faith in God, it is because of an inability to see the larger picture. I recommend people ask themselves: if our Creator can operate the whole universe with the assistance of the angelic hierarchies, wouldn't it make sense to trust this Source of all wisdom and love?

Prayer on a regular basis is important, not really for God's benefit but mainly for the effect it will have on your life. The best prayers are ones that *acknowledge* the gifts, love, and glory of the Creator. A person does not really have to ask for anything but only acknowledge that the love of the Creator is so great that the solutions, the help, the comfort have already been arranged.

Of course, there are occasions when one wants to pray for help for others. Still, the most powerful prayer is to acknowledge that help was already given according to the will of God. The problem arises when we want the response to be in a particular form and get upset if we don't see the results of prayer in the way we would like. This is an attitude of obstruction, and it will only lead to a feeling of separation between self and the Creator. We need to trust that God is present in our lives each day, even if we do not see things occurring the way we would like. Just because the angelic underworld is more obvious and seems to have a louder voice does not mean that God is not right beside us every step of the way as long as we honor Him.

Every time an incident occurs that seems tragic, practice thinking about what possible good could eventually come of the event despite the presence of rebellious influences. When you read the newspaper or hear the news, start seeing events on a higher level. Ask yourself questions: What will people learn from this event? What spiritual quality might be developed in those who just hear of the incident?

When we learn to think in broader terms about such tragedies, one day we realize that our faith has become incredibly strong. The reason is that with the type of thinking I suggest, you will be in the position of defending God—to yourself most of all.

Find a time when you can practice your faith in new ways. If you believe in Jesus Christ, then choose a period of time when you will forbid yourself to judge others. This was a new spiritual law that has yet to be fulfilled. If you are Buddhist, pick a month, or year, and consciously develop an aspect of the Eight-fold Path. If you are of the Jewish faith, select a period of time when you will no longer break a particular commandment, and infuse this law into your consciousness. The same should be done with any religion. If you don't have a particular affiliation but consider yourself to be spiritual, as so many people do in these times, select some tenet of one of the religions that you feel came from God. Then live it for a specific period of time. You may find that it becomes part of your life, which is a wonderful possibility. Then know that the reason our world is unable to get along is that *good people with good ideas believe on the larger scale but don't set aside time, focus, and action for the smaller parts of a life built on faith.*

I have a favorite image of how little we understand faith in other people and in ourselves. Many times we see it and consider that people with strong faith are ignoring the facts. My response is to remember the way in which a tiny ant colony can literally move a mountain. Yes, you might say it is instinct. However, to the ants the potential for failure must be overwhelming when they start out. *Yet, they do it.* Isn't it possible for humanity to achieve near-impossible tasks also?

One cautionary reminder: expanding your faith does not mean buying a lottery ticket and believing, because of God's participation in your life and your willingness to share the money, that you will win. Such activities have the potential to bind one to illusionary thinking and eventually to expand greed rather than faith. Expanding your faith means living in such a way that you continually reaffirm the presence of God. As long as you consciously work to align your life with God in all areas, the Creator and His angels will take care of you. All that you could possibly need will be provided even if it is not the way you might desire. *Remember that the heavens are much wiser than we could ever hope to become.*

Start your day with an acknowledgment of the presence of God in your life, and you will find a lasting ability to meet the people and events that you encounter. Spend a few minutes of quiet time before rising for the day. Use it as a time to reaffirm your trust in the Creator and the angels who work on behalf of the light.

TAKE THE REAL JOURNEY

The striving toward enlightenment should become a deeply religious experience on a personal level. This means that one should not seek knowledge or light for one's own purpose but as part of actions taken to strengthen one's devotion to God. If this is not the theme of the process, then any enlightenment or visionary experience is fleeting and possibly illusionary. One should also realize that, as soon as the desire develops for visionary experiences, they will cease or become instruments of illusion.

REMEMBER MICHAEL

Allow the image of Archangel Michael's strength and selfless service to God, which led him to defend the heavens against the rebellious angels, to bring forth a devotional feeling in your heart toward God. This is an extremely powerful image that can transform our planetary life. Bring this image into focus whenever you feel overwhelmed by life. Remember that God's love for you is even greater than that which Michael has for the Creator.

LEARN THE REAL STORY

There is much that is not known about the relationship of Christ to the Archangel Michael and the realm of the sun. With an open mind learn everything you can about the Christ as a spiritual being, and you will discover incredible truths that transcend any religious interpretations or bias. Once you make the decision to explore this subject, you will receive direct guidance from your own angel. Become knowledgeable about the relationship of the Archangel Michael to Christ.

REMEMBER, ONE GOD ONLY

If your career or family is your main focus in life, you have been honoring another god instead of the Creator. Remember that your career is only for a certain number of years; your family responsibilities are only for this lifetime, sometimes less. However, your relationship to God is eternal. *There can be no other priority.*

Think over the work you have chosen to do to create economic stability for yourself and perhaps for others. Do you spend time during a working day thinking about getting ahead rather than how you can serve God? Are you more frightened of offending your supervisor than of making a poor choice on your inner spiritual journey? Do you rate your successes by the praise of fellow workers or a supervisor, by the amount of salary, or by how your work is in alignment with spiritual law? Do you wonder how you can find a career that will contribute to the betterment of the world? Does your career require you to be dishonest, such as by working on weekends when you inwardly know you should be resting or being with relatives? Are your decisions based on acquisition of money and influence or on what is morally imperative?

If any of these questions gives you pause, you may need to realign your career. Design the kind of work that will enable you to balance your life and permit you to take your heavenly consciousness with you as you enter the boardroom or drive a bus, without becoming an obnoxious persuader of the supremacy of your faith.

When it comes to family life, a good test of whether you have made it into a false god is to ask yourself if you could leave it in a moment if it was the will of the Creator or if you could be at peace if the family was no longer part of your future if this was the will of God. If you can answer "yes" to these questions, then you know that the most important relationship in your existence is the one with the Creator and none other. Once attention is focused primarily on *this* relationship, a true and healthy perspective develops for the other areas of your life that establishes lasting harmony.

I remember having discussions with my parents during my early twenties about the call I had received to work spiritually to help humanity. Frequently they did not understand why I would want to dedicate my life to helping people understand about heaven if I refused to become a minister, nun, or other official religious figure. They doubted that I could ever make a career out of my love for God and the spiritual wisdom I was gaining daily about angels and the uncommonly known aspects of the various religions.

When I visited my parents on weekends, my father and I spent hours talking in the garage while he puttered at his workbench. After long periods of conversing about very deep spiritual truths, he would look at me with a half smile and say, "That's all well and good. It's wonderful you are interested in such things and that you like helping other people. But how will you ever work in the business world?" Each time I would answer the same way, by stating that if I worked for God I would serve Him in *whatever* world I was in and *whatever* task I was given. It was over a quarter of a century later that my father honored me by acknowledging that I had, indeed, successfully demonstrated this principle by my life. *It is only humanity that erases the presence of the Divine from our work.*

BE PREPARED FOR A SPECIAL VISITOR

There are many people in this century who have experienced a figure who appeared to them, spoke words of comfort, and then seemed to disappear. Sometimes these incidents can be actual people who are inspired to act at a specific time. Other times one's own angel might be making an appearance. On certain occasions, however, it might actually be the Etheric Christ Himself who appears around the world.

Prepare yourself each day in all ways in everything you do, and you will be able to respond as the heavens would hope.

OPENING THE DOOR AT LAST

As you read through the last section on heaven's requests, if you found yourself wanting to respond and help the hierarchies of angels, it is time to open the door to the heaven within. You will find that this not only creates a threshold through which the angels can reach you but also through which you can perceive the realms of heaven. If you choose to keep the door closed, the future of our civilization is at stake.

Chapter Eight

WORKING FOR THE
ANGELS

The most wonderful happening during the past few years is the increase in the number of persons who not only believe in angels but are also sincerely working in whatever way they can to contribute to the transformation of our world. The numbers will grow. As each soul takes upon itself an inner commitment to work on its inner life and then becomes directly connected to God's will through the angels, there is more possibility that we will be able to step over the abyss rather than fall into it.

People volunteering to work with the angels of God ask me what can be done when specific events occur, like a terrorist bombing in which a relative dies, or when there is some global problem they feel is going to impact on all humanity. The answer I give most frequently is compatible with the visions of Mary that have occurred during this century: *it is time to pray.* Aside from prayer and the inner work requested by the angels for all humanity to undergo, as explained in the preceding chapter, there are certain activities that the heavens recommend for anyone seeking to assist the angels of God:

DETERMINE YOUR ANGELIC LIFEWORK

Over the years, one of the most frequent questions I hear is: how can one discover the career or profession that is in line with one's spiritual destiny? My answer is that the contribution of your work life should always arise from those activities which you truly love. *When one offers these actions to be done in the name of God alone, there can be no greater insurance that one is doing the right thing.*

Think over your work life. If you are doing what is closest to your heart, then it serves the angels and proper remuneration will always be provided. For example, if you are being divided by a desire to work for money while living in a city and would rather live as a fisherman you are doing both yourself and the world a *disservice* by not making a change. It is only *attachment* to materialism that prevents our opening to new experiences that might, in the long run, provide far more security and benefit to our spiritual and economic health. I suggest doing an analysis of those areas of your life where your heart sings and creating a career around such work. If you do not, then your energy and happiness will fade away as you demonstrate lack of faith in the Creator's wisdom and ability to provide for you once you have committed your life to Him.

There are so many people I know who are happy today because they took a chance and aligned their lives with the work they truly love. I remember the many executives who moved from city life to the seashore to write or start their own businesses, the doctor who took up painting, the housewives who opened stores. Whatever the interest they had, it *originated* with the types of tasks they love to do. The time is never too late to make a change. If you are active in a career that gives you the feeling of joy and the realization that you are also helping God, then you are in line with your destiny. It will only get better and better.

Should you be confused about what direction to take, remember that your angel will not direct you because that would mean the loss of your free will. Your guardian angel wants you to use your own initiative. Once you make a decision, the guardian angel can bring help and signs that indicate the decision was in keeping with your destiny. If it was not, then you will feel a long silence which is the angel's way of encouraging you to change your mind before plans become actions. Always know that the answer to the question of your lifework is something that will contribute to the betterment of human life. If it is at all destructive, then you are not working for God but for yourself.

ESTABLISH HEALTH ON ALL LEVELS

We often forget that the scale of health can be out of balance at either end: one is when we become overwhelmed with a current disease that fills all our waking hours, and the other is when all our waking time is directed toward remaining healthy. These conditions arise from a misplaced focus. The self has become more important than God. As a result, on the one hand, the health fanatic has chosen the body as a god deserving of most of his or her attention; on the other hand, the sick person has given over Divine power to a set of viruses, bacteria, or other encroaching illness.

Over and over again, it is the wise physician who remarks that lasting healing comes about almost of its own accord when the patient makes a decided shift in attitude.

When we become ill, it is our responsibility as angel workers to assess what area of our consciousness has gotten out of balance to the point where sickness could steal our attention. Sometimes the illness can be an impulse for change, for cleansing, or for a new way of life. When this happens, it is good.

Above all do not venerate good health but recognize that it is a gift from God. *Never judge another person's soul by the nature of his physical health or appearance, or you may fall for an illusion.* The way to determine real health within yourself is a willingness to take action in the outer world to help others and to help God. If the body appears to be physically in order but the life remains focused on self, pleasure, or gaining the approval of others, the soul is in an unhealthy condition.

One of the most important aspects of health from the viewpoint of the angels is the quality of sleep that a person has consistently. This does not refer to the number of hours but to the ability of the soul to recharge the body during sleep and its accessibility to angelic realms while sleeping. The more a person translates outer actions from the realm of personal gain into an attitude of sincere generosity with thoughts, feelings, and deeds, the greater the level of entrance into the heavens during sleep. If during the day one's thoughts are filled with negativity or focused predominantly on material security, then during sleep the person cannot rise into the higher realms but stays strongly connected to the body. Many people remark how healing seems to come to them after a particularly deep sleep.

Avoid, at all costs, thinking about negative topics just before going to sleep. Instead, it is an excellent time to pray for others and to hold the image that you are being lifted by your angel into spiritual realms for true rejuvenation.

Travel in a Sacred Way

One of the important tasks that the heavens will usually ask of a soul committed to service is to travel quite a bit. The reason for this is that something special happens when a person who is conscious of angels meets another person who is not conscious of angels. The unconscious person's guardian angel becomes inspired by the angel of the person who is actively working for heaven. Many a time this interchange helps to lead a person back to their destiny or into a relationship that the angel thinks is important for spiritual development.

When you do travel, remember that you are representing the angels who are with you and act accordingly. Be kind and gracious and patient toward all with whom you are in contact. I know how difficult travel can be, especially air travel these days. Now when I make a journey, I not only bless the plane when I get on it but I also start praying for the flight the moment I book it, including all technical support, crew, pilots, baggage handlers, and food. When you arrive at the airport and release the luggage, ask God to assign an angel to escort the piece until its return to your hands. Believe me, it does work.

On the plane when you dine, be sure to bless your food. Should you decide to sleep, know that it is an unnatural form of sleep, which is why one rarely feels refreshed when getting off a plane. The reason is that your etheric body, or life force body, cannot travel as fast as the physical body and is forced to lag behind, stretching out in the space behind the physical body, sometimes for a *considerable* distance. Upon landing, it takes a long time for the etheric body to integrate again with the physical body after traveling at high speeds. This is the explanation for the strange tiredness felt after flying.

On the plane you can ask your angel to help contain your own etheric body and also protect you from the experience of riding in the force fields of persons sitting in front of you.

If you start to feel upset or have strange thoughts when flying, it may be due to riding in someone else's negative energy field.

This extension of the etheric body when flying makes one very sleepy. Rather than trying to sleep, unless the length of time requires it, I recommend using the whole trip as a time to think of angels in whose realms you are flying at the moment. Look out the window for clouds in the shape of angels, and use the time to become closer to God. Listen to music that awakens your devotional life, and pray for all those persons who are in your life. If you travel this way, you will survive the most difficult of flights. Naturally, avoid drinking any alcohol, as if you were about to enter meditation and prayer.

Upon entering a hotel room, do not stay there if you feel cramped or depressed when you walk into the room. It may be that rebellious angelic forces were active in the room due to arguments, thoughts, feelings, or actions of people who had stayed there before you. If you have no choice, then pray to God to cleanse the room immediately and let the light of your own guardian angel fill the space. Then you will feel rested and protected.

Lastly, pay attention to anyone who is assigned near you on a plane, boat, or dining room, and realize that the angels might have been working to introduce you to one another. This does not mean go looking for these occasions, but when someone does address you, don't cut him or her off until you are sure inside that your guardian angel had not arranged it with that person's guardian angel. So many times we miss opportunities to connect with old friends who we don't recognize in this life.

HELP ANGELS AT THE THRESHOLD

Birth and death are two of the most important areas where you can contribute not only to the world around you but also help souls who have left their bodies and souls who are about to enter their bodies.

If someone has died, there is little you can do to

minimize the shock and grief. However, you can help comfort the soul by encouraging the friends and relatives left behind to ask their guardian angels to assist the angel of the person who has died. Birth and death are two of the major functions of the guardian angel. When you ask your angel to help another person's angel, the assistance is pure and receives the blessing of God. Personal desire is removed. You can also ask that your own guardian angel help the angels of the grieving ones who are dealing with the death.

During the first three days after death, the soul is undergoing a review process with its guardian angel. Life is being reviewed in backward order. It is a time when the soul is seeking to understand the major achievements of the life and what is left unfinished. To assist the soul who has made the transition, there are some things you can do:

1. Read spiritual material to the soul as if the person were standing in the room with you. Pick material that had meaning to the person, and if you do not have that piece of knowledge, then find something that explains about the realms of angels and will speak of devotion to God. Use parts of the Bible or other sacred texts that are important to the individual.

2. You might assemble photographs of the person's lifetime and observe the changes. See if you can sense the purpose of the life.

3. An activity, which is actually comforting for those who grieve, is to make a list of the person's fa-

vorite places to go, music, art, poetry, people he or she admired, food that was enjoyed, goals that may have been set, or anything that helps describe the personality that was developed during the lifetime.

4. Permit the image to rest in mind that the soul has completed his or her work, even if it seems departure was too soon.

In the case of young children and babies, often these are souls who have come in for a short visit and have work to do in the heavenly realms. The most important thing to do is to remain in a state of inner balance which allows for grieving but keeps extreme emotionalism contained. The reason for this is that it becomes easier for the soul that has left its body to come close to family and friends to provide comfort and say a last good-bye with the help of the angels. When the grieving ones hold their heads facing upward, looking at the skies rather than focusing on the loss, the soul will speak in the stillness of their hearts.

If you believe in angels, then help those who grieve to receive comfort from the heavens. Help them to see the image of angels welcoming the soul into the spheres along with other friends and relatives who are already in those realms. When we help to transform the process of grief, we must do this delicately and without imposing our own will. If you can do nothing, at least become aware of the many angels present during the process of death, right up until any funeral or memorial service. Even silent acknowledgment of their presence will help all persons involved.

As we grieve over the death of a human as he or she enters the spiritual realm after completing a life experience, so also do the angels and other souls in the heavens experience grief when a soul is being born on earth. What is considered death, in our present realm, is a birth back into the spiritual world and a time for joyful welcoming of the soul that has left its body. Likewise, when a baby is born and we are filled with joy, we are facing a soul that sometimes is grieving because it has left the loftier realms of heaven and agreed to enter into the denseness of life. Oftentimes, this is the reason for the sad and frantic cries of certain babies even when all physical needs have been met. The soul that has descended is longing for the spiritual realm and is not yet comfortable with having a physical body.

I have found that it is effective to encourage the parents to speak directly to the new baby and promise to help the soul adjust to the difficulties of life and complete the purpose for which the soul has come. If that is done shortly after birth, amazing changes can be seen. A special strength seems to come to the baby. Another perspective to keep is that the baby has a guardian angel who is especially active during the early years of life. If you do not know how to help a young one, ask your angel to connect you to the guardian angel of the child, and eventually the image or sometimes the direct knowledge of what to do will come to you.

Whether you are dealing with a birth or a death, remember that they are both threshold experiences and thus *holy events*. The gates of heaven are open for souls on these occasions, and if we are aware, we will experience the light of heaven shining in the midst of these transitions.

FOCUS ON YOUR NATION'S SPIRITUAL PURPOSE

Working with the guardian angel also involves helping the archangel who oversees the nation in which one lives. In addition to their global influences, the archangels have areas of the earth for which they are responsible. As explained in chapter three, in the United States we have been under the stern guidance of the archangel Uriel since the late 1980s. The activities of archangels have no connection with politics but only with the work of individuals who have specific jobs that will affect the destiny of the nation.

If you would like to help align the country with the destiny as protected by the guardian angel of the country, known as the archangel, there are some things you can do: Study the history of the nation and begin to view it from a spiritual perspective. Envision the archangel bringing in light from the sun and spreading it throughout the nation, not only to institutions but also to individuals and their guardian angels so that they might make the right choice from a heavenly viewpoint. So many times it is difficult for the archangel to help the nation because of an inability of people to receive inspiration from the angels. The decisions that affect our nation need to be truly inspired rather than contrived for political or economic gain.

I also recommend praying for the transformation of certain national institutions. Ask your guardian angel to help connect the institution or part of government with the archangel for purposes of expanding the good. Believe that your prayer has been received by God and is under response despite outer appearances. Many times changes are not easily visible until quite a bit later.

Periodically I have held prayer gatherings for our nation. It is amazing how the lives of participants seem to lift as their focus becomes selfless and positive about the future. Everyone would select a particular problem with society that meant something to them personally and which they would like to transform. Whatever was selected, the participant would pray for the transformation of that problem and, if possible, track developments in the media. Personal desires should not be part of this process. Prayers should only be directed to God, asking that the nation be aligned with its true destiny and that help be given to overcome opposition forces.

Those of us in the United States need to remember that Uriel wants the outer world to be a true reflection of the inner world. If our nation is filled with darkness within, then there will be outer hardships of equal force. If we can increase our inner light as a nation, then outer conditions will improve. There is no way, for example, that we can transform problems of environmental pollution if we do not remove the pollution in our thoughts and feelings. *The toxic waste that is truly threatening our existence is the influence of negative and materialistic thinking.*

An infusion of spiritual light into the souls of decision makers is required in order for any national problem to be healed.

REJECT FALSE MEDIA

For years, I have recommended that people who are interested in seriously working with the angels of God act responsibly in terms of discerning truth from illusion in the media. Very little activity on the part of good forces is ever reported, supposedly because it is more enticing and lucrative to report deeds accomplished as a result of the influences of rebellious angels. When you hear the news, consider it a status report on the success of the underworld, but do not be disheartened. The successes of the forces of good are not honored or reported with anywhere near the depth and intensity as are acts of moral imbalance.

When you see a violent act or tragedy, seek to lift it to a higher perspective by remembering that all the truth has not been provided. No one knows the real background except God and the guardian angels involved. Whatever you do, avoid developing a numb response that accepts horrors of human nature as commonplace and therefore acceptable. A good example would be walking by the television and listening to a news report on a recent crime and thinking, "Oh, well, one more burglary...." Each time we hear of such news, we should reaffirm that the rebellious angels are *not* going to win in the long run. When you do hear occasional reports of good events, realize that the media have just barely covered it because of their addiction to reporting the negative. Tremendous numbers of people do real acts of kindness, honesty, and generosity every day all around the world, but the media refuse to believe that people are as interested in hearing about these heavenly successes as they are in hearing about murder, crime, violence, drugs, and distortion in our societies.

Very rarely will television and print media (other than those programs and periodicals that are religious in nature) report on subjects that relate to goodness if the parties are spiritually vocal. The message has not been released that it is time to report on spiritual activities that transcend specific religions. People are hungry to hear about the successes of the angels of God in containing the darkness in our world even though the media are blind to this.

Lastly, pray for the members of the media that you like. Pray that they will be guided by their angels to report the truth and only the truth.

DESIGN STRATEGIES FOR THE DENSITY OF LIFE

As we enter the next century, there will be increasing numbers of souls who find it difficult to live around other people who think and act in a negative manner, or who are attached to materialism. Some people have already begun to feel this and experience a growing contrast between living spiritually and dealing with non-spiritually oriented communities, businesses, and people. It becomes increasingly uncomfortable, as if one were wearing scratchy clothing. Since these differences are going to become more accentuated as a division becomes apparent between those persons aligned with God and those who are under the influence of the rebellious angels, especially Ahriman, a strengthening process is needed to endure life.

A good idea is to plan ahead carefully when dealing with outer world demands, and remember that God's will can enter into your interaction if you ask for this. Know yourself and what you need to maintain balance.

I learned a few years ago that with each increasing year, and as I worked more with the realms of heaven, I would feel battered if I went to a city unprepared. Eventually, I began to feel this way about going to a shopping center and then finally a department store. Now I find it difficult to go to the supermarket. When I return home, I often feel very drained. This experience will be happening to more souls as the conflict intensifies between the forces of rebellion and the angels of God.

The solution is to prepare for these adventures into areas where sales of material items are loaded with the energy of selling and greed, by maintaining a balance and walking slowly. Rather than rushing through such areas, go quietly, with serenity, and the draining influence will be minimized. A good image is to think of yourself moving with the graceful and leisurely pace of a member of royalty. I suggest this image because it is hard for us to think of a king or queen dashing about. And remember, it was the tortoise, not the hare, that won the race.

Finally, learn the pleasure of not agreeing to buy items. I have practiced this many times by going through a shopping center determined to leave with no purchases. Try this in the grocery store. The experience is powerful. Eventually you will feel that it is much more difficult for the forces of materialism to tempt you. Then, when you really want to purchase something, it will come from a level of higher conscious choice, not as a result of someone else's influence. This will strengthen your soul immensely and free your thinking in a way that is part of the work of Archangel Michael.

ASSIST IN TIMES OF EARTH DISASTERS

People who serve the angels of God are particularly aware of earth traumas. Not only is physical aid necessary but *spiritual aid is also essential*. What is important is to recognize that whether it is an earthquake, a tornado, a volcano, or another natural disaster, such an event is directly connected to human consciousness. Earth changes are a way the planet reestablishes a balance after human negativity has reached an unbearable level. Sometimes the realignment occurs in one part of the world due to events or group thinking in another part. We must remember that the earth is alive and is a conscious being even if we cannot comprehend it in our usual way of defining the inner world by materialistic means.

Here is how you can help. When there is a hurricane reported, think of whether there is some part of your life where your emotions are swirling around and might even become a violent force. If this does not apply to you, then just by your becoming aware of the connection, you help in minimizing damage. If there is a volcanic eruption, think about areas in your life or the lives of those around you that have the potential to become volatile and to explode. When earthquakes occur, view them as times when the heavens are trying to shake humanity awake so that spiritual balance can be achieved. Usually after any type of disaster such as an earthquake there is a broad expanse of awakened compassion and activities of sincere charity. Our world would be so much safer if we could learn to avoid these earth events by lifting our consciousness. Let your love stream into the earth. It will be received and will help.

If you are wondering what is the best thing you can do to help the people who suffered or were traumatized by a natural disaster, ask your guardian angel to help the guardian angels of the people involved. This is much more effective than demonstrating excessive emotional responses. Of course, do everything possible on the physical level, such as sending food, money, and other items of need. Your own angel will guide you in what to give if you ask.

Stand Against Ahrimanic Technology

Become conscious of those times when you are supposed to agree to interacting with a computer rather than a human being and refuse. Over the years we have gradually relinquished our communications to machines to the point where we can have a conversation with a mechanical voice to discuss important personal and business matters. This has been accepted as the norm in our society, and increasingly we are being told what to do by mechanical voices merely to increase profits for companies that want to cut down on personnel or avoid direct human interaction. Voice mail is now widespread. Many of us know how frequently a situation exists when people are conversing for days, and even weeks, through answering machines. The most difficult one for me is the digitized responses which instruct you to interact through numbers. This is making us into computers day by day. Whenever possible, find a way to interact with a human rather than a machine.

Another area where the angels could use your assistance is in supporting the experience of hearing real music created from original non-electronic instruments, such as the violin, trumpet, piano, and harp, or the human voice. Synthetic music may be entertaining, but it is not true sound, and it will not uplift the human soul. Rather, it will pull one too strongly into the human body even if the music is intended to portray the realms of heaven.

Find a way to support live concerts on real instruments for both children and adults. At such events, not only is there the enjoyment of listening to music together, but the angels of God are also very active. They delight when there is a recital, a symphony concert, or a string quartet. If you look carefully with your spirit, you will be able to see or at least feel the presence of the angels working to help in the performance.

In addition, you might consider learning how to sing or play a musical instrument, not for professional reasons but as a way to interact with the angels and to enjoy sound. Recently I started playing my flute again. I know how much the angels love to have their birds receive love offerings of even the simplest sounds. When I sit outside and play my flute it is exhilarating. I treasure these moments when I can return to the heaven-sent birds even the most meager reflection of the beautiful music they offer me throughout the year.

Help Bring Back the Manners

It is a sad commentary that our society is almost empty of signs of the true manners that are an essential part of spiritual work. Etiquette is connected to the intention of showing respect for one another, not to the indication of status. Unfortunately, even on the highest levels of human interaction, we have lost the meaning of graciousness.

When I speak about the return of manners, I do not mean false or insincere behavior that masks our feelings. What I mean is behaving as if the other person is also connected to the angels of God.

People speak rudely to one another, they become dangerous on the road if a few seconds are lost in driving from place to place, restaurant manners are at an all-time low, and children appear in public frequently as wild animals spewing out willful bad behavior and language. Businesspeople are rude on the phone, and customers demanding action treat businesspeople as if they were less than human. Spend a few days observing in your area, and you will see this. Be aware also of the few people who are by nature very tolerant and polite.

We need to put back the manners in our human interaction. I know that the angels work much better if humans show respect for one another. It is unnecessary to let loose the snakes of our bad behavior when we are in public, no matter how tired we are. Yes, sometimes there may be occasions when the other party is not listening to you even though he or she heard every word. The situation may require "squeaking" a bit to get results, but in your mind there should be respect for the other person and an acknowledgment that he or she is also created by God. You can never be absolutely sure that the person you just interacted with was an angel.

Therefore, I suggest all angel workers go on a campaign to lift the level of etiquette in our society, from courtesy in driving to expression of gratitude to people we interact with. As we begin to act like beings trained by the heavens rather than the underworld, our lives will radiate a lovely graciousness into the world around.

Everyone should find what etiquette means for them and stick by it. I know that in today's busy world it can be difficult to do it all the way we like; but try. Sadly, I must say that I have run across many angel workers who are perhaps the rudest people I have seen, and I did not understand it until I realized that inflated egos have brought about their lack of etiquette and in some cases total insensitivity. We must become more patient and not fall into the planetary mind that says we can have answers to our demands within the next ten seconds.

People have become addicted to instant gratification, and nowadays if a person doesn't receive a response by return mail, he or she becomes irate. Why can't we slow down a little? Angel workers cannot live so fast that they are trying to eat a seven course meal with the speed of taking a pill.

Remember Your Vulnerability

The fact that you have a sincere interest in helping the angels of God can make you a prime target for forces of illusion to detour your path of work. One of the weakest areas, where one would not expect there to be influence, is frequently in the desire to help others. It is because it is a desire that it makes you vulnerable, not because you have determined to help. If you maintain an attitude of detachment from whatever you are doing, with no ego gratification about how nice it feels to help others, then you are protected. Also, it is important to keep any efforts to assist *confidential*. A typical problem is when someone has made a sincere grant to a college or sent planeloads of food to a disaster area and then publicizes it in the media. Personal gain should not be connected to the impulse to help others. The only acknowledgment should be that God and the angels are responding through humans to help in a specific situation. Sadly, it is very difficult for people to forgo recognition of what they have done on behalf of God, and thus the deed's value becomes lessened in terms of heaven. *We must not take credit for that which was God's design all along.*

This is why most of the real holy ones, or saints, are very rarely identified in this world. Seek not the honor of men but the honor of God.

Chapter Nine

WHICH FUTURE WILL
WE CHOOSE?

We are coming very close to the end of time available for humanity to take responsibility for the direction in which we have moved in this past century and the urgent need to realign with God *immediately.*

The contents of this chapter may seem impossible to believe. It is not my task to convince you. Pictures of two different futures are presented. During my lifetime working with the angels of God, I have been given these images for release at the right time. They are offered in order to encourage your individual commitment to the Creator. Or perhaps it is time to renew your dedication.

The first series of images only hints at the darkened world we will live in *if the commitment is not made* and our societies remain under the powers of illusion and materialism. Many of these images may be quite alarming as you read and realize the ugliness of the abyss in front of us. Some of the beginnings that

I have described have already made their appearance. Above all, the condition presented should not be a source of fear, but *a deterrent to apathy.*

The second series of images, "A Future of Hope," conveys only an inkling of the beautiful world of peace that is possible if we ask for the Creator's help. His angels are ready and waiting to lift our lives away from the grip of the adversary forces. We need only to ask for help. In order to know what to ask for, we must behold the truth.

Our Creator can help us live in a new world right here on planet earth. He awaits our choice as we move closer and closer to the abyss.

If we ignore the call of the angels of God, our future can be described with these images:

- Terrible diseases will develop more than ever before that the medical profession will be unable to diagnose, cure, or even treat.

- There will be an increase in arthritic illnesses and viruses, unless we develop ways to release our rigid thinking caused by fear.

- There will be growing numbers of people who will seem to be walking machines, without any human warmth or consciousness.

- There will be extensive isolation experienced by people as a result of a growing fear of interacting with others. This will lead most people to communicate electronically without personal contact.

- There will be a vast amount of deformed life-styles due to the lack of positive angelic connections during sleep. This effect will result in people fearing the spiritual world while also venerating physical life in a distorted way that will lead to extreme attempts to preserve the body at death, in hopes of using it later. Such practices deny the wisdom and will of God in setting the time for natural completion of a life.

- There will be an increasing acceptance of acts which violate spiritual laws, such as dishonesty, adultery, parental abuse, and so forth. There will be an increase in the difficulty of telling truth from illusion because of the distortions implanted in the subconscious through movies and television during the past fifty years.

- There will be a growing veneration for the absurd, in particular the spiritually deformed side-shows that have become popular on television. Our society currently praises immoral actions by giving them national attention. In some cases, money is provided for speaking of the depths of depravity. More focus is placed on such people and lifestyles than on others who contribute to the betterment of human life. The media will increasingly seek exhibitionism of spiritual malfunctions.

- People will lose the ability to remember, and the loss will dim their consciousness. This in turn will limit the amount of spiritual transformation, which requires an awakened consciousness.

• Because of the hardening of the feeling nature under the influence of the rebellious angels, the relationship between humanity and the animals will change drastically. Pets will become a thing of the past as the relationship deteriorates and is banned from society. We will be unable to love and care for animals as we do now.

• The plant world will also become aggressive and deformed. The earth will be inundated with strangling vines and carnivorous plants. Fruits will not be produced by trees and bushes, and beautiful flowers will be a rarity. Birds will cease to sing because there is no longer a rising sun. Songbirds will gradually disappear, leaving only scavengers.

• Huge, hostile insects will overwhelm the earth.

• A blue sky will become a thing of the past because of widespread practices of witchcraft and other pagan rituals that venerate darkness and the light of the moon. People will forget about the sun and concentrate completely on the moon because it will actually seem lighter at night. As a result time schedules and sleep patterns will be disturbed.

• Souls born during this dark time when humanity serves the rebellious angels will be those who like the negative environment of the earth. They will be easy students of the rebellious forces. Souls that are spiritually evolved will remain in the heavens until such time as their good deeds will be more effective. Only very strong good souls will descend, as hidden rescuers. Their task will be the preservation of the memory of God.

- Ugliness of soul will no longer be hidden but will become physically visible around the eyes. What we now define as physical beauty will not be sustained. People will age quickly unless they give to others from their early years onward. No amount of medicine or surgery will have a lasting effect on this.

- Sexual acts will happen in public as an accepted norm and for entertainment value.

- The planet will be inhabited by thousands of roaming bands of ruthless violent murderers who devastate any area they enter. No one will attempt to stop them. Gang wars of the twentieth century will be comparable to a grain of sand to the whole beach. Such will be the level of spiritual ugliness that the populace will be paralyzed with fear.

- People who go to psychics will end up going to them endlessly, similar to the way drug addicts become controlled by the substance. Even if they receive false information, it won't matter to them. The impulse to return and be told *what one wants to hear* will be the only form of comfort that people will have.

- People will walk around speaking about the things they want to do but are unable to accomplish. This is similar to a condition recognizable in the mentally unbalanced person. There will be increasing experiences of this state because people did not put into *action* earlier in life the priorities they know to be true.

- There will be continual loss of inner freedom, to the point of no creative incentive, original thinking, or independent action. People will follow an inner programming of self-automation. Governmental systems will reflect the people's desires by endorsing mechanistic controls to prevent the use of free will. All actions will be monitored in private as well as public.

- Libraries will not exist except through electronic means. Paper books will become a thing of the past. The selection of allowable items on computers will be monitored and edited by the government to prevent any mention of spiritual knowledge. It will be explained that this is in the best interest of the citizens, and the justification will be the history of past wars based on religion, freedom, or ideas.

- The subject of God will not be permitted nor will people be able to read, or even think, about the angels of God, especially Archangel Michael. All churches, temples, and mosques will be closed *without any opposition* by the people, who will have forgotten about God or no longer care.

- The workers of God will withdraw from public access to protect spiritual knowledge for the future. People will not be able to locate comforting counselors anywhere.

- People will become so confused they cannot recognize goodness any longer.

- As computers replace human beings in so many areas, it will become harder to tell if a person is a computer or a computer is a person.

- Deep restful sleep will be impossible because of terrible phantoms attacking people on the astral plane. Instead, people will go into a drugged trance while they rest. Because of the density of the soul's consciousness, guardian angels will be unable to lift souls into heaven during sleep. As a result, the physical body will not rejuvenate properly, and life forces will deteriorate unless falsely strengthened by the forces of darkness. This activity will bind souls to the underworld.

- Birth and death will no longer be viewed as belonging to the heavens but as something to be determined and controlled completely by humanity. Births will have to be registered before conception, or the child will be destroyed. No person will be allowed to live past a certain age but will go to a processing center. Body parts will be harvested. The life span will be lowered repeatedly, to the mid-thirties, to obtain the best workers and limit the drain on food reserves which will also be shrinking. Even at this early age, people will look quite advanced in years due to the negative influences and lack of spiritual sun.

- In order to obtain something they want, people will think it natural to annihilate the life of another without feeling any guilt. Human corpses will be everywhere, with no system to handle them effectively and respectfully.

- The ability to distinguish friend from foe will be lost. Everyone will appear as if they were an enemy.

- Those who seek after music, beauty, and refinement will be punished by a society that demands coarseness.

- Individuality will be punished by public reprimands. People will be instructed to have the same hairstyles and clothing.

- Historic documents will be changed so that the memory of spiritual events, biblical times, and other knowledge about God is removed.

- The earth itself will shudder from this abyss experience and will shake off the negativity by means of tremendous devastation on a planetary scale. Very minute areas of the earth will be protected, along with sufficient nature forces and elementals to preserve certain plants and animals. These locations have never been revealed by anyone and will not be known for thousands of years until such time as civilization has been rebuilt on the principle of love.

It is not necessary to describe the *complete* nightmare of hardship that will manifest if the warning call of heaven is once again ignored. The angels are working so hard to make their presence felt because they have special orders from God to help us make our commitment *before it is too late*. If we choose the heavenly alternative, then Archangel Michael will liberate humanity, and specific interventions will occur to remove the rebellious influence of the angels of darkness.

If the majority of our civilization starts to behave in a way that honors our God of Creation, the angels will build a bridge of light over the abyss that will lead us into a new condition of life. Here are some of the potentials that await us if we use our free will now, this moment, to commit, or recommit, to the love, wisdom, and will of God.

A FUTURE OF HOPE

- From the moment of birth, each soul will be recognized as an aspect of God which has come to the earth accompanied by angels. Mothers who give birth will be honored for their sacrifice of flesh and life force that they have given to create life.

- Society will highly reward anyone who cares for a child. Any souls born with physical limitations will be treated as if they were saints coming to visit and will be given very loving special treatment from before the birth itself and throughout life.

- Parents who cannot give birth on their own will see it as a call to work with other children and will locate young souls without parents.

- Behavior problems and learning disorders will not exist, and children will feel loved and very happy. They will be open to the realms of heaven and know how to use spiritual sight to see angels.

- Education of the child will be seen as a sacred process, and those permitted to teach children will only be adults who have learned to love fully and also are very knowledgeable about the workings of the universe and the spiritual realms. Students will be taught how to assess the quality of their own learning by how they are able to apply it in the outer world. Teachers will emphasize the integration of moral life with the decision process as a foundation for all future work.

- Prayer in whatever religious manner, or nonreligious manner, will be respected and encouraged as a way to connect with true knowledge. Religious intolerance will not exist.

- Medical practitioners will study the interaction of spiritual forces with the human body, including anatomy from a cosmic view, before learning the traditional sciences. They will be highly trained in the use of natural substances to balance the human form. No surgery or treatments will be undertaken with a patient, except in emergencies, without close examination of the spiritual and physical processes involved. Medical doctors will routinely work with the patient's guardian angel to gain correct diagnosis and treatment. As a result of this interaction, the medical establishment will regain true humility. The goal for medical practitioners will be to serve God as agents for healing.

- There will be no need for policemen or military forces. Crimes and wars will gradually become a thing of the past. Instead, there will be "shepherds" to help travelers and others in public access areas. They will provide information on resources and be connected to the fire and rescue personnel.

- Entertainment will be filled with stories that inspire hope and provide actual knowledge about the world of nature and the cosmos as well as biographical material on souls who have contributed to society. Violence will not be accepted in entertainment or sports because it will be viewed as socially disgraceful.

- Nations around the world will maintain their own cultures, which will be respected by other nations. Visitors to any country will be treated with honor as citizen ambassadors of their own land.

- Airline travel will be transformed completely by designers with a background in spiritual knowledge of the human being. This will minimize shock to the life forces and impact of the plane on the natural world. These changes will mean fewer passengers and redesigned seats so that one does not have to ride in the aura of the person in front as it flows back into the seat behind it. Pilots will be trained to acknowledge the angelic realms through which the plane would have to fly. The plane's design will create a walking and stretching area for longer flights. Oxygen will be viewed as equally important as fuel. Airlines will no longer save fuel on long flights by reducing the amount of fresh air circulated throughout the cabin. Eventually, aircraft will operate by the use of magnetic forces.

- The young in society will be appreciated and encouraged to learn spiritual knowledge. They will be given tasks that utilize youthful energy but will not be venerated because of it.

- Teenagers will be filled with positive impulses for the future and will have more respect for creative independent thinking than for the forces of peer pressure which demand multiple copies of the thoughts, feelings, and actions of others.

- Elders in society will be treated as wise ones to whom much respect should be given. A result will be the positive reception of elders. They will participate more fully in society and will be able to share their wisdom and experience.

- All business agreements will be reviewed for compliance with spiritual principles before they are signed. Lawsuits will not be necessary. Conflicts that arise will be resolved by sages, or "wise ones," in the community, chosen by virtue of their past deeds. Divine law will have precedence over human law.

- When people have to make a decision, they will pray to God over the matter and consult with their guardian angel. Thus, errors in life will be at a minimum, enabling individuals to spend more time on activities that will contribute to society.

- National income tax systems will be transformed into a gifting process incorporating annual reports from individuals documenting what they have done for others and how they were directly a help to society during the year. There will be national honor lists. People will be tax free for a period of time due to the generous way they lived during the year. This policy will be one of the most transforming influences in society. The program will be monitored by local sages to whom one submits reports and receives endorsement before sending in the annual filing for the gift system. Dishonesty will be impossible because of the documentation and review process. Evidence of greed or attempts to hide financial wealth for the purpose of personal gain will lead to receiving reprimands and mandatory spiritual training as well as dispersal of funds to sources that operate in a balanced way.

- The economic world will be balanced as businesses dedicate their income to help society. Greed in the investment world will be viewed as shameful. Accumulation of wealth used to energize spiritual projects that help the work of the angels of God will be respected.

- Any actions that violate spiritual law will be viewed as caused by an imbalance in the thinking, feeling, and will systems within the individual. People who are responsible for violations will be handled lovingly and rebalanced through knowledge of the spiritual nature of humanity and the universe.

- Scientists will have the ability to understand the link between God and manifestation. As a result, completely new revelations in physics, health, astronomy, geology, and biology will occur. Scientists will work closely with the sages and other people who are well trained in spiritual knowledge.

- The energy of positive thoughts will be so beneficial to the environment that plants will grow healthy and strong when in the presence of a person because they will be receiving an energy similar to the energy of the sun, radiating from the aura of the person. This knowledge will be developed in a beneficial way to help certain parts of the earth replenish food supplies from the depletion of the twentieth century.

- Research money for healing will be directed toward balancing the physical body with the soul and spirit rather than the development of curative drugs.

- People will become healthier and remain that way, allowing for occasional accidental traumas to the body. Hospitals as we know them will not exist; there will be houses of balance where care will be given. Surgery will be rarely performed; when it is necessary, anesthesia will be done with sound, rather than drugs.

- Souls will be born who bring with them specific gifts to eradicate illness.

- People will naturally have the capacity to see the consequences of their actions before enacting them and thus avoid unnecessary error. The imaginative process will be highly purified and reliable, as will be the ability to receive true Divine inspiration.

- The spiritual attitude of a person will release a beautiful scent into the world as they walk, making perfume unnecessary. This fragrance will be different for each person and impossible to replicate chemically. It will reflect their moral development and will be referred to as the *scent of God*.

Chapter Ten

THE PETALS OF THE ROSE

The angels come closer to us when we look upward with a determined will to fill our consciousness with the light of God. This process is rarely done in a flash. Inspiration comes to us like lightning, but the pathway to a heavenly consciousness is a continual series of developments in which we learn more about the Divine and more about ourselves.

The angelic hierarchies would like us to establish a better relationship with them. I suggest that we begin preparations for the future by offering the heavens a *spiritual rose*. Each petal consists of a Divine quality important to God to receive from us through the angelic hierarchies. Each is essential for the future of humanity. The act of focusing on these aspects of Divine love creates a wonderful light which will radiate from your soul. Your guardian angel will transport this beautiful offering to the Creator.

The seven petals are discussed in sequence but

should be viewed as a circular process of development that involves working with each aspect of the rose to some degree all at the same time.

These spiritual petals are *responsibility, humility, truthfulness, courage, selflessness, honor, and delight.*

1. RESPONSIBILITY

Many years ago I redefined the word "responsibility" as "the ability to respond according to the will of God." Our guardian angels are very good at this. We need to learn from the angels the importance of being responsible and how to act this way. Picture, for example, that your guardian angel decided to take a day off or got tired of escorting you or said to God that it was tired of your attitude and wanted to work with another person. This does not happen in the heavens. *Assignments are assignments until completed.*

Picture the angelic hierarchies who help with motion in the universe, the dynameis, as they keep the planets in rotation. What would happen if they decided to take a rest on some cloud and see what humanity would do?

These images may be amusing, but they also point out that a guardian angel does not sleep and has no moment in consciousness when it is not working to serve God. We humans require sleep and relaxation and food, which are not necessities for the angels. They don't complain. What they do know is about rhythms and cycles. They are aware that to succeed at a task requires following certain cycles on which the universe is based, either a giving out or a pulling in.

Even the rotation of the planets is achieved by a combination of these motions similar to when you spin a ball in your hand.

Over the years I have met many individuals who are filled with good intentions but somehow have difficulty with responding to a commitment they have made. Other souls are overly concerned with how they are personally responsible for the needs of others *while ignoring the perfect care of the angels* assigned to these people. Both extremes need to be balanced so that our stairway to heaven becomes strong with deeds that reflect a sincere willingness to act.

A good image to explain the cosmic aspects of responsibility is this:

> *You exist because God thought you into being. All that is manifest exists because of the original thought sent forth into manifestation. As soon as God ceases to hold the thought of anything, it ceases. Therefore, God has been responsibly maintaining the thought of your existence as a spirit and soul from the very moment of your creation. Think of the level of responsibility and commitment involved in this loving deed. The goal of many lifetimes is to become conscious of that original thought and to fulfill the potential that is within it out of your free will.*

Your guardian angel protects and maintains the memory of that original thought with Divine instruction to guide you through experiences and opportunities that will fulfill your unique potential.

2. HUMILITY

When one truly understands the nature of humility it becomes clear why so little of it is manifest in the world even among angel workers. More often than I would like, I receive calls or letters from people who are convinced that they are actually angels and that they have a special mission to heal the world. It is, of course, possible. However, there is a greater likelihood that these individuals feel connected to the angels and receive some ego satisfaction in thinking they are actually angels. My experience has shown that even holy persons do not identify who they are unless it is absolutely necessary in order to accomplish God's work. The way highly evolved souls are identified is by the deeds they accomplish in the world around them and the selfless manner in which they accomplish those deeds.

Such persons who are highly advanced know who they are, and why they are on the earth. There is no reason for them to trumpet their work to souls of lesser development. Anyone of equal level of spiritual consciousness will identify them immediately by the deeds they accomplish and the inspiration they provide others.

If you were to look closely, you would also find that they had an enormous amount of humility which was the reason for their success. The humility arises from a deep recognition that it was a simple task to fulfill the will of God at each step and that it was much easier to inwardly acknowledge that the only one who was really working was God—as if God Himself was moving throughout His own creation. To have this consciousness prevents one from having the kind of egotism that many people interested in spiritual things might have. The worst type of egotism is the hidden variety. The best type of humility, however, is also the kind that operates deep inside a person and is often very hard to see.

This reminds me of the 1960s when I came across people who would be drifting through life with a glazed look, speaking softly, bowing humbly, and by all appearances completely humble in awaiting the word of God. Yet if you looked deep inside, there was a tremendous force of egotism that inspired those people to openly declare to the world how spiritual they were.

I would gladly prefer to converse with a strong but clear personality that even might appear to the outer world self-absorbed but inwardly walked the path of quiet humility. I know that such persons are much more real in their commitment to God. No matter how fiery or vibrant their personality, they are absent from harmful intent.

Humility leads us away from the temptation to have power over others or to compete against another person. It does not make us weak or like a patsy who can be walked over. On the contrary, if one develops real humility, it is not in relationship to other human beings but in relationship to God. That attitude enables the individual to have remarkable strength that can make it difficult for the outer world to see the true depth of this spiritual quality.

A good image to explain the importance of humility is that of the flowers in the garden:

> *The little peony does not shout to the other flowers how wonderful and unique its blooms are this year and how much better the colors than the petals of the rose. And the rose, when it is blooming, doesn't announce to the peonies and the other flowers what a perfect scent it has created. All the flowers are busy looking to the sunlight, pulling themselves from the darkness of earth and lifting their green bodies high enough so that they can bring forth their gifts. For a rose to take credit for its scent would be ridiculous because it knows that it is a gift from God to be relayed to humanity. That is why flowers rejoice when we admire the beauty they deliver to our souls from heaven.*

Likewise, if we work with the angels, humility enables us to deliver the love of God and share its scent out in the world.

3. TRUTHFULNESS

In today's world it is especially hard to identify truth and to be completely true in all ways as much as we would like. So often society has set up areas of our life where truth is allowed to be flexible.

For example, a road sign will say that the speed limit is 65 m.p.h., but people often drive much faster than accepted laws permit. There is a basic dishonesty when we do this if we do not seek changes in laws we do not wish to follow. The lives of others can be affected by the lack of truthful behavior, whether it is that of a person who is openly untruthful or one who is so fearful of being somewhere late (sometimes rushing to do nothing) that he injures others on the highway. Every day people's lives are put in jeopardy by these bumper-kissing drivers.

We must ask ourselves, however, if we believe in following the law as posted. If not, then one needs to take action. Become active to change the group consensus that has allowed for this or any other limitation. If, yes, you do believe in obeying the laws of automobile travel, *your actions become untruthful* the moment you exceed the speed limit.

The example is to show how easy it is for us to violate our sense of truth.

The angels want us, above all, to be true to ourselves, to be truthful inwardly and truthful before God. It is only through the manifestation of the truth of who we are that real beauty can shine. Most of the world's people go around with makeup on their souls in addition to their faces. Even men hide behind a facade of appearances that are pleasing and acceptable to the business world. If a person decides that it is necessary to compromise, that can be done without spiritual harm *only if one is truthful to oneself about what is being done.* Sometimes it is necessary to wear a costume or put clown makeup on our face in order to achieve the results. The problem arises, however, when the performer believes he is the clown and will not remove the makeup and clothes either for himself or for other people.

I think that truthfulness is very much like a musical instrument when it is in tune. However, when one is untruthful the note is played off-key and one wonders whether or not the musician is aware of the sound he or she is making. What was to have been a pure sound is released as a painful screech. The noise that is made does not blend with the sounds of other symphony musicians unless they are all out of tune. Then there is chaos.

Each day as we rise, we need to adjust any imbalances. If, as the hours wear on, we tire and start to hear screeches again, it is time to reconnect with God and the truth of who we are.

What can be done if we are not sure about our truth? Ask God to let your angel heal any illusions about yourself and to strengthen your ability to live the truth in all areas of life. This does not mean to feel instantly guilty if you are now aware of how many areas of your life hold little compromises with the truth. Instead, work to overcome the unnecessary untruths little by little each day.

One way to start the process is to stop flattering people with compliments if you are seeking to bring them pleasure when, in truth, whatever it was you were going to comment on did not warrant such praise. Save your praise for times when you sincerely feel it, and the person will truly be appreciative. When you have started on this process, you will realize how much of the world is lulled to sleep by the drug of false approval. Then there will rise in your soul a thirst for only true and valid experiences.

After this has developed, a wonderful opening occurs. Your angel will begin to guide you toward experiencing how truth will lead to the revelation of real beauty. You will hunger for manifestations of beauty that reflect a connection to spiritual truths. And as these two components come together, you will seek *only* to work in areas of goodness filled with spiritually conscious people.

In our world there is so much dishonesty that in order to do the simplest tasks we must negotiate through false advertisements, false media reports, false labeling on the food we purchase, and products that do not live up to their claims.

It is time for us all to encourage the world to honor truth more than lies and dishonesty. At present, we reward dishonesty by allowing areas of political activity to stray from the truth. We also reward it by placing the emphasis in our society on packaging rather than contents. Too much of the economic system is built on manipulation and deception. It is just as sad as the old shell game played on a sidewalk. We fall victim to dishonesty because we don't demand honest expression and a consciousness filled with spiritual truth.

The major process of being truthful to oneself involves being true to God. It is not likely that your angel will lead you into heavenly realms until you face the depth of your commitment to God.

An image that might be helpful is this:

You have a spiritual mailbox and perhaps have been unable to live your truth. Each time that occurs, the number on your box changes, causing the spiritual blessings addressed to you to be undeliverable. God does not reroute his blessings if you are the cause of the interference. However, if you remain true to yourself, the heavens can find you even if the outer world seems not to approve of who you are. Always choose to be truthful in the highest sense, and you will find that goodness and beauty accompany you throughout life.

4. COURAGE

Most of us have had moments in our lives when we used courage to reach an important destination that required travel through dangerous areas. If you think back, the reason you were able to summon up courage was that you were determined to get where you were headed.

This spiritual quality is essential in learning to work with the heavens because there are many tests and trials that you will come across. These trials have the potential of expanding your soul. However, they also will bring forth from within you the ability to stand fast and strong when confronted with fear.

Many heroes on the battlefield, when acclaimed for acts of courage, will say that, on the contrary, they did not feel courage; rather, they felt fear while being impelled to take action. It is this *overriding of paralysis* that is the important aspect to courage that our civilization needs to develop. We will continue to face situations in our lives where fear is experienced, and to deny it will not help. We can, instead, recognize that fear is an activity of the rebellious angels. This recognition will counteract the paralyzing effect of fear. Once the negative source of such emotions is discovered, the process of loosening the grip of fear has started.

An example of how fear can distort our lives and prevent us from connecting with a positive future is in the area of relationships. One of the main reasons that communication between people breaks down has to do with fear. Husbands and wives cease interacting when they fear the response of the other. Children stop talking with parents when they fear that there will be no support for or agreement with their viewpoint or requests. Employees will not speak about changes they perceive as necessary because they fear loss of a job. Politicians fear rejection at the voting booth, and this prevents them from taking all the actions that they would truly like to take to help the nation. The media are filled with fear that the populace will not be interested or not support them financially if they communicate about God other than to report specific religious events or write about spiritual issues in a disparaging way. The result of all this is a massive problem in communications on all levels in our civilization.

If we are to understand courage, we need to view it from the standpoint of the heavens. To the angels, courage is nothing more than *taking action for a truth perceived.* The Archangel Michael has demonstrated the quality of heavenly courage through his defense of God against the rebellious angels. He does this with a strength that emanates from the heart, the seat of all truth. He knows that there is need for action and so he takes it.

Many of us find it difficult to take such actions when we perceive a truth; this is an activity that we can develop that will help the realms of heaven. The world is filled with people who love God and who would want the world to be a better place. They struggle with the demands of their own circle of responsibility and lack the courage to go beyond. It is this extra stretch that is so valuable to the heavens, provided such acts of courage are based on spiritual truth.

The area where we could concentrate on developing courage is within our immediate family units and in our work environments. Find some aspect to your relationships where you are held back out of fear. Then remember this: *fear acts like an eraser that can remove the potential good designed for your future.*

Each time you lack courage, look to the truth of the situation. If it is painful or difficult, once you acknowledge it strength comes to face it. Each time you replace the fear with courage, even in little acts, you will feel the angels rejoice.

I have an example in my own life. Many years ago I realized I was actually frightened to open anything that came in an envelope. This was so irrational since I had no fear of the contents. It was the sight of the envelopes, or unopened mail, that bothered me.

This presented a problem because as the years went by I found ways to delay opening letters, even one with a check in it or perhaps a nice warm letter. One day I realized that the element of fear had insinuated its way into my communications and I had to do something. I prayed for clarity, strength, and courage to resolve the problem.

Gradually images entered my mind of an event in my teens while away at college when I mailed off an important letter to a gentleman friend. The memory returned of the morning I was about to take a major exam and passed by the mail baskets for the dorm. A letter addressed to me was sitting there. I opened it. Inside, unopened, was the letter I had mailed to my friend. These words were scrawled upon its face: "This is to inform you I have just become engaged to someone else." There had been no indication of this in our conversations, and I had just returned from a visit with him.

Obviously at that moment I was unable to respond to the pain of the incident because I had to start a critical exam in fifteen minutes. The memory went underground and became a vehicle for the rebellious angels to interfere in later years. The pain I experienced was not so much from the dissolution of the relationship but from the *way* it was done. He had shown the effects of lack of courage, and I knew that this lesson could be important in the future.

I began to realize that when I saw unopened envelopes, I was unconsciously remembering the pain of seeing my own unopened letter so many years ago. With the help of my angels, I knew that with courage

I could release this memory and replace it with a picture that each envelope held potential good and could be a message reflecting the love of heaven.

It is interesting that this incident of fear is common to many people, perhaps for different reasons than my own. Some individuals are fearful of bills or even too much junk mail. As the years have passed, I still work to transform that old fear. Now it is not the same. I approach each envelope with expectation that there may be a blessing in it, a treasure. It is happening. I am discovering wonderful little miracles. Even the envelopes are being transformed as people send letters with stars, angels, and even glitter all over the outside of the envelopes. Never have I seen such pretty mail on the outside as well as the inside. This transformation was successful because I used courage to remove the fear and replace it with awareness of the presence of God on all levels.

In our relationships, we do the same thing that I was doing when my fear of envelopes interfered with communication. We frequently avoid hearing what others are saying or pretend that it doesn't need attention. We also experience times when we try to communicate an important thought to another person, and they do not seem to receive it, similar to leaving an envelope unopened.

We need to encourage others to communicate truthfully with us and to be clear communicators ourselves. Perhaps it might also be a good idea to release positive pieces of communication to those we care about and create surprises in their lives. This may only involve telling someone about a quality he or she possesses that you finally recognize and appreciate.

An image of sunlight helps in understanding courage:

When you feel overwhelmed with a fear, the inner light has been diminished to some degree. Fear and courage cannot exist at the same place and at the same time. Where courage is, God is manifest. And the heart (le coeur in French) is active. Where fear exists, awareness of God has been removed and darkness descends. It is similar to the clouds in the sky that interfere with the rays of the sun that seek to warm and comfort us.

See yourself reaching up through the cloud obscuring your light, and take hold of a ray of sunshine. Bring it down through the cloud, and hold on to it. Sit quietly and take part of the sun ray under your arm, like a hose, and aim it straight at what you are worried about. Spray it with sunlight, and you will find that courage to act or to speak will come to you. Most important of all, you will have courage to change the situation.

Each time you reach up through the clouds and bring the sunlight into the realm of conflict and darkness, your action brings positive substance into the heavens for use by the angels of God.

5. SELFLESSNESS

One of the most wonderful petals on our spiritual rose is created from the healthiest attitude of soul—to be able to focus and act in such a way that what we do for the self does not overwhelm what we do for others, and what we do for others does not harm ourselves.

Practicing selflessness does not mean denying the existence of self. Rather it means creating a healthy relationship to the world around and not letting one's personality or ego abuse the world. It also means developing a new way of looking at others: seeing them as no lesser and no greater than oneself. Selflessness also has a connection with the age-old behavior policy known as the Golden Rule—*Do unto others as you would have them do unto you.* Part of the reason for the abyss which confronts us is that so many people have adopted the policy of self-first thinking. This attitude has led to a world filled with the results of selfishness on a grand scale. Think about this: how many times have you done what you thought was best for yourself first and then expected others to treat you with preference? It will not work. If you treat others as second best, they will treat you the exact same way. Before long, everyone is fighting one another to maintain first position.

Most people will say that they are selfless in their lives: a parent might think he or she has selflessly dedicated his or her life and work to children; an executive might think that he or she is devoted to the development of a business. Then there are other people who view themselves as selflessly giving their lives for an ideal or cause they believe in or for the healing of patients or the expansion of knowledge. These are not examples of the selflessness that the angels will treasure.

Instead, the selflessness of this petal arises from the conscious lessening of the small egoic self, the personality, to be replaced by the greater spiritual self that acknowledges the needs of all. This greater self has the ability to see with the eyes of heaven and knows the truth that as long as the focus is on the Divine, there is no need to harm the world around us in order to gain satisfaction for the personal ego. Naturally, with the establishment of a heavenly perspective, the ways to respond to needs for the real self will be made abundantly clear.

The subject of how to help the outer world while balancing needs for the self is riddled with prescriptions for success that are in direct opposition to selflessness on a spiritual level.

An example is the frequent statement made to people who help others and who seem to wear out. They are often told, "If you don't take care of yourself *first* you can't take care of others." On the surface, this sounds quite true and reasonable, and it provides the incentive for a person who may have overdone actions for others to direct attention onto their own life. The problem is that such thinking endorses a subtle form of selfishness. This might be compared to a person who has found himself among others who are starving. He has been bringing in shipments of food but now finds that when he opens the truck, all that is there is his own lunchbox. The people who endorse the above statement would be the ones to say he should get in his truck and eat his lunch by himself so that he can drive off and bring back more food.

The difficulty in this situation is that the lunchbox does not belong to him any more than the foodstuffs he was delivering. Even if only a few people could share from the contents of the lunchbox, he should share. This act of sharing when one has little to offer creates a space for the greater spiritual self to manifest. I believe this was one of the meanings behind the biblical parable of Jesus feeding the crowd of thousands with only a few fishes and loaves of bread.

We are not used to stepping aside from our little self when there is a possibility we will not get food, comfort, or money that we think we deserve. It is valuable to the angelic hierarchies when we develop a perspective that sees one's life in context with other lives and the activities of other areas of creation. Each time we step over our little self and think on a greater scale, we are reaffirming our connection to God and belief in the greater wisdom operating in our lives. If we rely upon our spiritual self rather than the little self, everything we could possibly need will be provided in accordance with the will of God. Would you want anything in your life *that God would not wish for you?* It is time to surrender the little self—which is the way to establish in your soul the quality of selflessness.

Here is an image that will help in the process of creating the petal of selflessness:

The natural world and your own body exist because of the selfless generosity of spiritual beings who gave of their own essence. Each day you are immersed in a substance that embodies the principle of selflessness: it is water. Without this heavenly substance our world would cease, as would your own life without either the ingestion of water or its release. A river must flow or all will die. We need the rain to allow itself to merge with air to form droplets that can fall as snow, ice, or rain. When we receive water into our bodies, it is symbolic of the selflessness of the spiritual world. True health is when this water can purify and sustain our bodies and the realms of nature. Water can take upon itself the power and will of God, should it withhold itself from a desert or unite with winds to create the fury of a hurricane. Whatever form the water takes, it gives of itself to respond to the intentions of Divine forces in nature. As we become selfless, for the sake of a greater self, we learn to respond to the will and purpose of Creation.

As you develop this petal on your spiritual rose, the highest angels are pleased because your selflessness is helping to fulfill the will of God.

6. HONOR

This petal is perhaps the one that gives an extra sweetness to our spiritual flower. It is time to return honor to our relationships and to all the areas where we interact. When we honor another human being by silently recognizing that we are addressing a portion of God dwelling in the spirit of that person, even if the person's actions may not reflect this, we send forth a trumpet call to the heavens. This is because when we acknowledge the presence of God in people, in nature, or active in the events we experience, we strengthen the works of the angels and improve our relationship to the realms of heaven.

The importance of practicing honor is basic to all successful family relationships, including our relationship to the Divine. Religions, as well as spiritual practices that are not formalized, include this basic principle of honor. If followed, this quality will *uplift* a person inwardly, both the recipient and the person expressing honor. This is because one cannot practice spiritual honor without looking upward toward the heavens. Each time this is done, *an angel is aware.*

To begin developing honor as an offering to the angelic hierarchies you can dwell on this image:

> *The angels of heaven gather around the throne of God and sing praises, "Glory, Glory, Glory." With each utterance the Light of God beams throughout Creation, pulsating to the heartbeat of the Divine Originator. The angels on each level offer praise and honor to the hierarchy above them, sending waves of honor right to the highest heavens. The music of the spheres that can be heard is none other than*

the voices of the angels expressing honor to the Creator. When you practice honor among humans, you take on the activity of angels. It will enable the spiritual hierarchies to come especially close to humanity. Most of all, this leads to the human voice blending with the sounds of the angels singing in honor of God. There can be no sweeter sound heard anywhere.

As you develop this petal, walk forward honoring the presence of God everywhere, and you will be accompanied by many angels.

7. DELIGHT

The last of the seven petals is very important. The angelic hierarchies rarely see this quality offered by humanity, so they treasure it when it is given.

The secret of this quality is in its name, *de-* and *light.* This means "of light." In everything we do, in every aspect of our lives, in our thinking and our feelings, *all areas,* we need to infuse those areas with the light of God. If we do this, we will experience a sense of bliss that is the other meaning of delight, a wonderful sense of joy.

This quality is valued by the angels because it is so very special when humanity uses its free will to replace the energy of darkness with the Light of God, especially out of love. Each time a person does this in his or her own life, it is cause for the angels to rejoice. The Creator is at last becoming the central focus in the life of a human; this means that the guardian angel, and other angels above, will experience a heavenly blessing, for *their work has been successful.*

To maintain the image of this seventh petal, think that:

> *The Creator does not rest, nor sleep, nor frolic in the realms of heaven with His angels. He is busy maintaining the focus which enables everything to exist. Yet when you experience delight, He also experiences delight, and this is why: our God seeks to please us, to bring us more happiness than we could ever comprehend. If God were to experience agony, it would be caused by not being able to explain to His Creation the reason behind everything and why there are times when things seem unbearable. But when we humans consciously seek to fill our lives with His Light, God experiences a form of pleasure that can only be granted by humans. When you find ways to help the angels and to transform the darkness, the Creator is well pleased. This offering is received into the heavens and leads to a beautiful image of the angels being deeply moved by the choice that was made. In addition to angels singing in praise of God, something else occurs. God whispers love directly into the heart of each human being. The most perfect union of all can occur on a conscious level. The Creator will merge your light and His Light together. Your identity will remain but be surrounded by the glory of God's love.*

IN CONCLUSION

As you work on these seven qualities, you will find your life changing. There is extraordinary spiritual strength that comes to a person who offers his or her spiritual work to the heavens. This rose, when created by you, will form a link between your head and heart and will inspire actions reflective of the highest within.

The petals should be developed all at the same time, rather than your waiting until one is completed before starting on a second quality. Perhaps you might even draw a rose, or paint one as you develop the petals. The rose is an ancient symbol that has many meanings, depending on the color. Red has to do with love and the passion of life, one of the gifts of God. The white rose has a connection with the angelic realms and the purifying action of service to God. Perhaps your rose is yellow, or pink, or some other exquisite color. Keep the picture of it in your mind and turn to it when you need comfort. It will be there.

Many people have actually smelled the mysterious scent of roses in a room. Often this is the presence of angelic ones. The human who perceives it has his or her spiritual senses heightened. We are able to offer to the heavens a similar blessing that will be equally pleasurable for the realm of the angels.

Let's send spiritual roses created out of our will and love for God. It is time for the heavens to receive a response to their calls: *yes, we will align with the Creator.*

But the ship was now in the midst of the sea, tossed with waves: for the wind was contrary. And in the fourth watch of the night Jesus went unto them, walking on the sea. And when the disciples saw him walking on the sea, they were troubled, saying, It is a spirit, and they cried out for fear. But straightway Jesus spake unto them, saying, Be of good cheer; it is I; be not afraid. And Peter answered him and said, Lord, if it be thou, bid me to come unto thee on the water. And he said, Come. And when Peter was come down out of the ship, he walked on the water.

—MATTHEW 14:24–29

About the Author

K. Martin-Kuri is an artist and public speaker and president of Twenty-Eight Angels, Inc. You may reach her by writing to her at P.O. Box 116, Free Union, Virginia 92240.

Threefold being: Pg. 80

1. Nervous system ∞ thinking process
2. Lungs relate to - feeling part
3. will system "'" — limbs + metabolic
                              processes

evaluate spiritual obstacles in
these three categories

Mary, Isis, Sophia, Eve   Pg 54

Kyrio means "Lord"